CALIFORNIA
LAND OF MANY DREAMS

First English edition published by Colour Library Books
© 1983 Illustrations and Text: Colour Library International Ltd.
  99 Park Avenue, New York, N.Y. 10016, U.S.A.
This edition is published by Crescent Books
Distributed by Crown Publishers, Inc.
hgfedcba
Colour separations by Llovet S.A., Barcelona, Spain.
Printed and bound in Barcelona, Spain by Cayfosa and Eurobinder.
ISBN 0 517 414864
All rights reserved
CRESCENT 1983

Dep. Leg. B. 40.115/83

CALIFORNIA
LAND OF MANY DREAMS

Text by Margaret Shakespeare

Produced by
TED SMART and DAVID GIBBON

CRESCENT BOOKS

California is known even to the most casual observer as the land where anything can happen. It can and it does. Somehow in this modern world we seem to believe that California is *the* place for the bizarre, the gaudy, the unusual, the eccentric and whatever just doesn't fit anywhere else. Take a stroll on Hollywood Boulevard. You're likely to notice an array of odd characters flaunting their colorful lifestyles; or proselytizing scientologists, with their clipboards and leaflets, signing up new followers; or the quiet unassuming shops of theatrical memorabilia, out-of-print books and stocks of 8 x 10 glossies of old character actors. They coexist oddly all along the same blocks. Breeze into Musso and Frank's Grill, with its crisply laundered white table linen, formally attired waiters, and roomy banquette – a little bit of old Hollywood still alive. Head north up Highland to the Hollywood Bowl, that larger-than-life amphitheater where jazz great Hubert Lawes and classical master Jean Pierre Rampal played their famous flutes together for the first time. Drive down to Watts District and have a long walk around the Towers constructed from cement and bits of shells, broken tiles, bottle glass, and other junk – the remarkable lifework of Simon Rodia (1920-1954). Though they are so different, these many features combine to form a unique society that could only exist in this Pacific Coast state.

California by its very history is a land of diversity, a place where the juxtaposition of the unlikely with the just-like-everybody-else is not only possible, but a way of life. Flower children flocked to Haight-Ashbury in the 1960s and before them a teeming Beat generation found a California haven. So did the Theosophists who settled in the Ojai Valley in the 1920s. And the evangelist Aimee Semple McPherson whose Los Angeles congregation seemed to grow in relation to the scandalous publicity she created for herself. Religious sects espousing any of a range of beliefs have always been able to make a home in California. So have dozens of ethnic groups. In Los Angeles alone, you can visit communities of Mexicans, blacks, Jews, Japanese, and Chinese, large enough to be cities unto themselves.

These people find a variety of ways to earn a living. They farm, manufacture, bank, cook, practice, make movies. And they play – at tennis, hang gliding, sun-bathing, sailing, surfing, skiing, jogging, aerobic dancing. And they all do a lot of driving just to get to work and play, not to mention driving purely for its own sake. The population is probably the most mobile bunch of people in the world, and the most fanatic about their vehicles. If you want to escape cars – and that hazardous California by-product, smog (which costs $250 million a year in damage to crops alone) – your best bet is the steamer from Long Beach or San Pedro to Catalina Island where cars are forbidden; and go off-season, midweek if possible.

But what of the land before there were automobiles, smog, and people to make their individual and collective ways? Before man began to devise and arrange his own villages, towns, and cities in California, what was the setting nature provided? Just exactly what did those 158,693 square miles of California contain?

For an easy and pleasant introduction to Californian geography drive up the coast from Los Angeles to San Francisco. I don't have to say, "pick a pretty day", because chances are almost any day of the year will do nicely. Plan that the trip will take about eight hours, without stopovers, and stay on State Route 1 (Pacific Coast Highway). The road twists and winds and climbs steeply and narrows, like the mountain highway it is, and in places traffic can be reduced to a crawl, but never mind. On the right-hand side you'll pass sun-drenched towns or lush forests that continue to ascend craggy inclines, while off to the left rolls the majestic Pacific Ocean, sparkling in the sun and dashing to meet the rocky shore. Enjoy and savor some of the most glorious views California, or any other state, has to offer. When you come to Big Sur country, about 50 miles north of San Luis Obispo, you will have entered one of the grandest and most alluring stretches along the coastal route. Even if camping out has never been appealing, you may find yourself pitching a tent and unrolling a sleeping bag; which is about the best way to revel in the glories of forest, mountain, and sea which abound in this uncommon country. Hike a trail into the wilds at Point Lobos State Reserve to behold the weathered, wind-gnarled Monterey cypresses and perhaps a sea otter or seal frolicking in the surf. The Reserve takes in 750 acres of sea floor as a refuge for wild plants and animals which flourish here in abund-ance. White sandy beaches alternate with rocky pali-sades in startling patterns and spring flowers cover fields with a crazy quilt of color and light.

A little farther north the exquisite historical towns of Carmel and Monterey border the lush shiny Monterey Bay. Monterey, especially, is all dressed up for show-and-sell to tourists, but it's been put together tastefully and with class. Shops and galleries occupy a restored Cannery Row, once a bustling sardine packing center. This is Steinbeck country and an area that has been, and still is, home to a number of writers and artists. You'll find charming Victorian inns and guest houses, picture postcard places with views to match, and plenty of excellent restaurants – lunch is even served at the house where John Steinbeck was born in Salinas, a town just inland from the Bay. Santa Cruz, less polished but comfortably charming, attracts more locals than tourists to its beaches. From here to San Francisco a few quaint little fishing towns decorate the coastline along State Route 1, and inland the San Mateo area grows fog-loving broccoli, artichokes, and Brussels sprouts. You know San Francisco looms ahead when dwellings of its suburbs start to clutter the horizon. And shortly you enter a cosmopolitan, urban environ-ment, curiously perched on some 40 abrupt hills and hugged on three sides by expanses of water.

Even in the city the country still shines through. On some counts Californians have tried to preserve many of the natural wonders and splendors of their land, while building to the future. San Francisco's Golden Gate Park boasts a roaming herd of buffalo. The La Brea Tar Pits, holding secrets of over a half million speci-mens of life, some preserved since the Ice Age, share Hancock Park with the Los Angeles County Art Museum in the midst of Wilshire Boulevard's nonstop 24-hours-a-day city traffic.

But more of the best, biggest, most astounding of California's natural assets remain as simple monu-ments to themselves. Consider the wealth of contrast, diversity, and grandeur that abounds in California's natural settings. Mount Whitney rises to 14,945 feet, the highest point in the contiguous U.S., tucked into the southern Sierra Nevada. Sixty miles southeast lies its antithesis, Death Valley, at 282 feet below sea level. All about is stashed the largest variety of minerals to be found in so small an area – gold, silver, copper, tin, lead, borax, and more. In counties north of San Francisco stand primeval forests of *Sequoia gigantea*, the giant redwood. Some of these trees tower 300 feet into the sky, making them the largest of all living things.

Lofty mountain peaks, low-lying deserts, craggy coast-lines and vast valleys present an astonishing collection of physiographic features: ranging from flourishing orange groves to Arctic flora, glaciers to volcanoes. The layout of the state, spanning 825 miles between its most distant points – Crescent City south to the opposite corner across from Yuma City, Arizona – encompasses two important chains of mountains: the rugged Sierra Nevada which outlines most of the eastern border, and the Coast Range. In between stretches the elongated

Central (Sacramento-San Joaquin) Valley, the largest agricultural area west of the Rockies. Water yielded by the Sierra Nevada nourishes the otherwise parched valley below. Ages ago, glaciers formed many of the 2,000 or so lakes and ponds pressed into the granite crags, the deepest and loveliest of which is Tahoe on the California-Nevada border. The gradient on the eastern edge of these imposing mountains is among the steepest on the continent and toughened the challenge for people crossing the continent to civilize the West. Not until 1869, when the transcontinental railroad was completed, did the rest of the world gain easy access to California.

The not so formidable Coast Range, which also catches water contributing to the alluvium of the Central Valley, is broken up by smaller valleys that sometimes extend right to the Pacific Ocean. Twelve thousand miles of coastline are marked as well by two great natural harbors – San Francisco and San Diego. The sea has long been a plentiful source of food and fuel, and made California the link between North America and the Far East. From the time that the first explorers and adventurers plundered the rich seas off the coast and took for themselves the whales, sea otters, seals, and other creatures, men dreamed about fortunes just waiting in the waters. Along the northern shores, Russian fur traders set up posts, which later grew into towns, where they had prime choice of ocean treasures and a vantage point for shipping.

Not all of California's natural heritage showers such blessings. Threat of major earthquake and the aftermath is living fact. In 1906, the city of San Francisco suffered such a disaster when the San Andreas Fault shifted. The Fault is a 600 mile long rift in the earth's crust, where two gigantic plates of rocks meet and constantly grind against each other. The tremors lasted a scant few minutes but buildings were ripped apart, streets blocked and the water mains destroyed. Fires from overturned stoves and cracked gas lines broke out and spread; there was not enough water to control the inferno. In the end, at least 125,000 people no longer had homes, hundreds more had died or were missing, 28,000 buildings had been reduced to rubble – in all $500 million of damage. We know it could happen again. Seismologists keep close watch on the faults that crisscross the state and record the tiny tremors that occur daily.

But earthquakes, or the threat of them, has not hindered the development or popularity of California. Perhaps nature's chief control over human endeavor has been the lack of navigable rivers which limits transportation, particularly of goods, to overland hauling or shipment by sea. Problems of getting a water supply to populated and agricultural areas became a task of many decades, but its accomplishment insured both urban growth and generous provision of food.

The promise of sunshine and temperate climate accounted in large part for the great population booms, especially the phenomenal increase in the size of Los Angeles from a nineteenth century pueblo to extraordinary twentieth century metropolis. In fact, it has been observed that, "the climate of southern California is equable: a commodity that can be labeled, priced and marketed. It is not something that you talk about, complain about, or guess about. On the contrary, it is the most consistent, the least paradoxical factor in the environment. Unlike climates the world over, it is predictable to the point of monotony. In its air-conditioned equability, it might well be called artificial. The climate is the region. It has attracted unlimited resources of manpower and wealth, made possible agricultural development... It has given the region its rare beauty." (Carey McWilliams in *Southern California Country*.) With more objectivity, Captain William Shaler, one of the first observers of California's natural attractions, commented: "The climate of California generally is dry and temperate, and remarkably healthy; on the western coast the sky is generally obscured by fogs and haze, but on the opposite side it is constantly clear; not a cloud to be seen, night or day. The northwest winds blow very strong eight months in the year, on the western coast; with very little interruption; the land breezes at that time are hardly perceptible; but in the winter months of January, February, and

March there are at times very high stakes from the southeast, which render most of the bays and harbours on the coast unsafe at that season."

In fact, California has two distinct seasons – dry and wet. The shifting of prevailing winds brings rainfall from September to April. During spring and summer months the hot, dry winds from the desert blow toward the ocean. To experience the gamut of California climates in a compact area, take the tramway up Mount San Jacinto near Palm Springs. In just 15 miles you will go from arid desert to lush pine forest. Overall, though, the mildness of the Pacific, which lies close to so much of the land, keeps California temperatures from reaching extremes of hot or cold.

Here, at land's end of America, millions have flocked for 400 years to a resplendent, varied frontier. It has always held a promise of the riches that nature could offer, as one British diplomat said in 1839: "Taking every circumstance into account, perhaps no country whatever can excel or hardly vie with California in natural advantages."

John Muir believed in the land as no person has before or since. Naturalist Muir, a Scottish immigrant, arrived in Yosemite Valley from Wisconsin, and stayed on to devote his life to study of the wilderness. He became an arch conservationist, preserver and chronicler of nature, and a legendary, if not controversial figure.

In 1864, just before John Muir reached what was to become his home, Congress had set aside the Yosemite Valley in the trust of the state of California as a wild preserve – the first federal action to save any part of America for posterity. The land had been ravaged when thousands of men descended upon the Sierra foothills during the early days of the gold rush. They grazed their livestock, hunted bighorn sheep and elk, and nearly drove many predatory species to extinction. Muir was the first person to come here and systematically record the secrets of the treacherous terrain. True, much of what he wrote – and he kept copious notes which were later published – expresses an unbridled passion for his subjects, but he also deduced a lot about geophysical history and compiled invaluable data. He observed the huge glaciers and noted exactly how ice had. shaped the granite chunks of Yosemite. Muir's fascination was caught by ghastly thunderstorms, quakes shaking the earth, and the habits of creatures – such as the ouzel, a bird that can 'fly' underwater.

He set himself up as a farmer in the valley, but often retreated to the high country for days at a time to study and write. The work that consumed his life became background for the conservation movement which ultimately resulted in the expansion of public preserves, and the transfer of Yosemite back to federal control in 1890 and its designation as a National Park. Muir himself initiated the Sierra Club whose goals embraced his own.

The Sierra Nevada now contains within its expanse eight National Forests and three National Parks. Finally, in 1964, almost one hundred years after Muir uncovered the beauties and wonders of Yosemite and the Sierra Nevada, the Wilderness Act guaranteed protection for designated wild acreage, defining it as land that retains "its primeval character and influence, without permanent improvements or human habitation and which generally appears to have been affected primarily by the forces of nature, with the imprint of man's work substantially unnoticeable", and that it should have "outstanding opportunities for solitude or a primitive and unconfined type of recreation."

Over eight million people a year visit the Wilderness in California. Many of them choose to remain tethered to the man-made conveniences of their roadside motels and automobiles – you can glimpse a lot of unbelievable scenery on a drive, especially through Yosemite National Park in the spring or autumn. Go to the Park headquarters in the Yosemite Valley first, where you can view Bridal Falls, Yosemite Falls, with 1,430 feet of upper falls, a cascade dropping 675 feet, and 370 feet of lower falls (these are the highest falls in North America); and the majestic El Capitan, the world's largest mass of visible granite. Route 120 bisects the

Park, taking you into the higher mountains and through alpine meadows. To do more exploring join up with a guided hiking expedition – some go out for a week at a time – from the Tuolumne Meadows area. Here lakes are hidden away just over the brow of a hill, amid great stands of pines. It is all guaranteed to take your breath away. Campsites for the adventuresome can be reserved in this area of the Park, and you can take a horse or bicycle into parts of the back country.

But for those with the spirit of John Muir, over 3,000 miles of footpaths and horse-riding trails wander through the peaks of the Sierra Nevada, covering three National Parks, and leading to meadows of wild flowers, crystal clear lakes, glacial settings; the realm of deer, mountain coyotes, cougars, and small scurrying rodents. Visit Kings Canyon National Park and Sequoia National Park – the two are adjacent and lie south of Yosemite – to experience the best and most rugged backpacking treks. The John Muir Trail starts in Yosemite at the edge of the Valley, runs through the John Muir Wilderness into Kings Canyon and goes right to the summit of Mount Whitney. The Trail will take you to the heart of back country at elevations never dipping below 7,500 feet, and in over 200 miles it never crosses a paved road. At Wallace Creek, just before arriving at Mount Whitney, the Trail meets with the High Sierra Trail, which leads through Sequoia National Park to the Great Forest. You are allowed to camp, fish, and, in some seasons, hunt certain animals. The Park Service does restrict the number of backpackers, horses and size of camping groups going into all of the Wilderness areas.

There are also a few mountain cabins, mostly occupied by people roughing it in the summer, near the tiny, almost forgotten, Sierra villages. Many of them don't have modern conveniences such as electricity, gas or telephones. Instead they have the most uncommon backyard in all of California, with an unending supply of surprises in color, sound, shape, and movement, and have clean, pure air to breathe.

You will notice, too, ski areas, downhill and touring –

some with lodges or other accommodation – scattered throughout the Sierra, most of them located north of Yosemite in the general vicinity of Lake Tahoe, second highest lake in the world. Snow caps the mountains year-round, and many lifts operate throughout the summer.

Stay in California country as long as you can: absorb it, feel it, listen to it, play in it, understand it, grow from it, learn from it. Once you have the experience you will always return. The land was here before all the rest and will remain brilliant, rich, and solid as the trends and styles, and people of civilization and urban life, come and go.

In 1542, the coast of California was discovered by Juan Rodriguez Cabrillo, a Portuguese in Spanish service, as he searched for the Northwest Passage. It was, however, to be over two centuries before the Spanish returned to make permanent settlements in the area, and during those intervening years Englishmen, Frenchmen, and Russians came and went on various expeditions: Sir Francis Drake ventured into Pacific waters in 1579, and a few years later, Thomas Cavendish captured a Spanish vessel laden with riches from the Orient near the California coast. All the adventurers sought a better or shorter route to the Far East, as well as scavenging the shores for whatever natural wealth lay in store. In 1768, King Charles of Spain finally made the annexation of the territory official, by ordering the colonization of California – partly in the interest of facilitating trade between Mexico and the Phillipines – but also to insure Spanish right to occupy the land. Indians, of course, had been inhabiting small villages up and down the coast, and in the valleys. They lived, though, in small bands, disconnected by geography, culture, and language, and had made little impact on the land itself. All that was to change with the establishment of missions, one of the key institutions in the Spanish plan for colonization.

Soldiers and priests had always gone together in efforts to advance Spanish land claims, and so Padre Junipero Serra went off to California, ostensibly to minister to

Indian souls, little knowing of, or planning to make, the historical impact which was the result of his venture. He received his assignment with apparent relish and enthusiasm, rounding up church bells, baptismal fonts, sacred utensils, vestments, and other church requisites he would need in the new land, and made the treacherous journey overland from Mexico in 1769. When his party arrived at what was to become San Diego, they were met by two ragged seafaring expeditions, which consisted of men from Mexico who were suffering and dying from scurvy. Not to be daunted, the padre, with all able-bodied survivors, continued his plans to found the mission of San Diego de Alcalá which took place in July 1769. Indians, first thieving and then attacking, brought further trial and difficulty to the tattered but hardy band of colonists. These months of tribulation, however, proved Padre Serra to be not only a missionary of zeal and determination in his quest to make a permanent religious settlement, but also a superb administrator whose effective ideas eventually became California legacy.

The mission at San Diego turned out to be the first in a chain of twenty-one such establishments extending up the coast along El Camino Real (The King's Highway) at about a day's journey (thirty miles) apart. The Franciscan padres always selected sites with three characteristics: good soil, a regular water supply, and a nearby Indian population. The fruitful land and water were essential, as they had to make each mission self-sufficient right away in order to survive. And the Indians, of course, figured as the primary focus in the overall scheme; as it turned out they provided most of the labor too. Padre Serra founded nine of these missions himself, setting up patterns for establishing the institution and for conducting everyday life therein. His foray after San Diego found the Spanish constructing a *presidio* (protective fortress) at San Carlos Borromeo de Monterey. Here he discovered that the mission house itself should be well-removed from the area of Spanish soldiers – who would gamble with the natives and lustily pursue women – if his religious influence was to be effective. So he located the next mission on the beautiful Carmel Bay, south of Monterey.

The padre received supplies and religious gifts for his missions from Mexico. He made an arduous return journey to Mexico in 1772-73, when he was received by the Viceroy – Antonio María Bucaréli – who asked the sensible, well-informed and dedicated Padre Serra for recommendations on further settlement of California. Many of the good padre's suggestions, including the mapping of land routes and the initiation of a transport service, were undertaken by Mexicans in their new territory and influenced later developments in California. Padre Serra returned to Mission San Diego de Alcalá in 1774, and then proceeded up the coast to take up his life's work again.

Mission San Juan Capistrano was founded in 1776 just south of present-day Los Angeles. Here, to this "Jewel of Missions", the legendary swallows still return every March 19th. San Buenaventura (founded 1782) was the last of Padre Serra's missions. He had also witnessed the building of four presidios to protect his cordon of missions, and the Viceroy effected his recommendation to found two pueblos; San José and Los Angeles.

Under Padre Lasuén, Serra's successor, the missions entered their most prosperous period, both materially and spiritually. He established nine more links in the El Camino Real chain and maintained careful administration over mission life. The Franciscans proved to be great farm managers and merchants. Soon they were overseeing what amounted to wealthy estates that produced healthy livestock, huge quantities of grain and thriving vineyards – so that the missions provided most of the foodstuffs for the whole territory and thus became the chief unit of economic as well as religious control in California. They constructed irrigation ditches and aqueducts, and each mission erected seemed to be more handsome and carefully designed than its predecessors. By now the Indians, whose salvation had been one of the original objects of this missionary movement, had become in many ways enslaved to it. The padres controlled the wealth which Indian labor had made for them. Decree finally came from Mexico that the missions should free the Indians and grant them a fair share of land and livestock. As of 1834, missions were to be secularized by law. They had been the principal unit of organization and economics in California for nearly seventy years.

Franciscan leadership produced flourishing autarchic agriculatural communities that existed for their own benefit, exploiting the good land of California for the first time in history. Life in and around the missions, while they thrived, improved enormously. The padres' assumption of control over the Indians meant teaching them the Spanish language, training them in various occupations and instilling their souls with Christian doctrine. Once attached to a mission they lived a workaday life – regimented by educational and industrial activities, ordered by religious services – but did maintain some freedom to indulge in singing, dancing, and other amusements. They were, in fact, encouraged to develop indigenous craftsmanship such as weaving and basketmaking. Indians, in turn, taught the Franciscans expert methods of drying and storing foods.

This trading and honing of skills shows up in artifacts from the mission era that remain today. While missions created great farms and wineries, they also manufactured tools necessary for the work, and furnishings for themselves and the community. Flax, wool and cotton could be woven, dyed and made into blankets, curtains and garments. Their looms became famous. Tanners made animal hides into clothing, furniture, saddles, stirrups, bridles, belts, gloves and structural supports – many items with intricate designs or braiding. In the early-nineteenth century they began turning from hand-powered grain mills to those operated by water or horses. So they not only grew more grain but made more flour too. Indian men learned to quarry stone, make sun-dried bricks and baked roofing tiles. They felled trees, and using the timber became excellent carpenters, making furniture, wine vats, confessionals, altars, and pulpits. The blacksmiths at San Fernando Rey became famous for their wrought-iron farm implements, locks, keys, spurs, scissors, cattle-brands, and bells.

With all this abundance of resources, California during the mission period still lacked a good, steady supply of building materials. Stone often had to be brought from some distance to the site of the new mission, and wood, in the south at least, was scarce. So they made use of clay, found in great quantity along the coast, for bricks, roofing tiles, pavements, and chimneys. The red colored bricks were flat, not more than two inches thick, and usually measured ten inches square. Adobe, made of clay and straw, proved to be a popular and durable building material too; usually they covered adobe walls with stucco to protect them against the elements. Walls of adobe had to be made quite thick – often five feet – since it's a substance that cannot bear a lot of pressure. Lime was made by burning either limestone or seashells and was used to keep wall surfaces whitewashed.

The Franciscans came to California trained as priests not architects. They were prepared to strive for the human good; little did they know that their ingenuity and zeal in struggling to establish Christianity in a new and rugged land would lead to a style and expression of architectural design and construction that would be admired by generations and held by Californians as the finest examples in their history. The ancestry of the mission style, now so important and prominent in California architectural annals, finds its roots in Spanish Cathedral construction going back to the Middle Ages – Romanesque and Gothic in the north of Spain, which flourished simultaneously with decorative Moorish influences in the south. Building style grew even more ornate in the Renaissance, shortly before the Spanish established themselves in Mexico. They transferred architectural design to the new land, making allowances only for differences in available construction materials; not much of the native Aztec design was incorporated. Work of local artisans and development of a Spanish-Mexican vernacular came gradually, but when it did the focus was on ornamentation. Domes, too, became a feature of Mexican architecture: domes appeared on secular and religious buildings, often covered with brightly glazed tiles. And the Spanish in Mexico lavishly bestowed churches with the riches of local mines.

The California padres inherited all the elaborate Mexican architectural style and, importantly, the trait of a very fine sense of proportion. Since their humble beginnings precluded use of skilled or artistic leaders, not to mention lack of stone and other decorative building materials, they concentrated on simple, clean lines which produced a new straightforward style of charm and practicality. To be sure, it features the Gothic and Romanesque influence of the Spanish (for example, arcaded cloisters) and Moorish focal points of detail (mostly found in church interiors) that Mexican architecture carried to an extreme.

Most all mission buildings have massive walls because of the available materials and the Franciscan tradition of constructing heavy, well-fortified edifices. The buttresses, featured in all mission churches, served the dual purpose of reinforcing high, long walls and the abutment of lateral thrusts of arches, vaults, or domes (most of the domes have since vanished). Arcaded cloisters, so similar to what can be seen in Spain, rest on substantial square piers, fine stone for support not being readily available. The lovely curved and pedimental gables, perhaps without Spanish precedent, emerged as a distinct stylistic development in mission architecture. Terraced bell towers, also, exist only in the California variety, though finishing details on the bell towers differ from mission to mission. Pierced belfries – starkly clean and simple – originated in California and influenced mission design in Texas and Mexico. Patios, of Moorish descent, brought to the western world the flavor of European gardens, and the ever-thrifty Franciscans incorporated them to serve utilitarian as well as artistic purposes in almost every instance.

Perhaps what remains most striking about the mission is the broad, unadorned exterior walls. Maybe this uncluttered architectural appearance resulted from a scarcity of artistic labor, but with it we see a cleanness of line, skill in execution, and ingenious adaption to the environment. For instance, the wide-spreading eaves and low-sloping, red-tiled roofs contended with both heavy rainfall and unrelenting sunshine, both typical California weather patterns. Freer artistic expression can be seen in the design of doors and windows. Some are rather plain openings with only a semicircular or elliptical head, while others, especially if they'd been able to get stone, feature decorative carvings or artistically conceived brick constructions. Sometimes they were trimmed or reinforced with ironwork forged by the blacksmiths. Almost all ornaments exhibit a wonderful mingling of Spanish and Indian motifs and craftsmanship. Crude wall paintings even adorn the interior walls of some missions.

Only one of California's original missions still serves the purpose of ministering to the Indians' spiritual needs. Most of the others stand as monuments to an era, a movement of dedication that bred a surprisingly auspicious cultural beginning to the state, and as superb examples of truly American architecture that has given impetus to many generations of design and artistic expression. The Mission Santa Barbara, the only one continuously under Franciscan control, has been photographed perhaps more than any other building in California. The "Queen of Missions" keeps a candle burning on the altar, as it has since its founding by Padre Serra in 1786.

Some of the missions did fall into disrepair, especially after they were secularized in the 1830s and 40s. Mexicans sold Mission La Purísima Concepción (founded 1787) at auction in 1845 for $1,000. Restoration by the Civilian Conservation Corps in the 1930s included molding over 100,000 bricks, just as the original Indian builders had done. Indian handiwork – wooden crucifixes, hand-hammered copper and silver altar pieces – is still in use at Mission Santa Inés, 35 miles north of Santa Barbara. Walls of this restored church, also home of California's first seminary, display a decorative mural. Padre Serra's fifth mission, San Luis Obispo de Tolosa (founded 1772), where roof tiles were first made, houses his vestments and other religious objects. Perhaps the most notable mural and arches can be seen at San Miguel Arcángel (founded 1797), ten miles north of Paso Robles. If you would like to attend a service in a mission setting, go to San Gabriel Arcángel (founded 1771) on the eastern edge of Los Angeles, famous also for its bells and religious museum. Padre Serra's first mission, San Diego de Alcalá, preserves his peaceful garden. The museum there contains artifacts of everyday mission life as well as religious articles.

The style of architecture created by the Franciscans has been often repeated in building design, not only in California, but throughout the southwest. Notice in cities and suburbs, the many wood and stucco homes with red-tiled, low-sloping roofs and arched windows or doorways. The first so-called mission revival occurred around 1890 with the construction of South Pacific railroad stations, famous for their broad, red roofs.

The Franciscans are recognized, too, for their toils in the fields and vineyards, as beginning the great multibillion dollar industries of California – agriculture and viticulture.

California feeds one out of every ten Americans. That's enough farming to make agriculture, together with attendant businesses, the state's largest and most important industry, employing one out of every three workers and grossing more than $12 billion annually. Over 64,000 diversified farms produce about 200 crops, 48 of which lead national production statistics. Fresno County alone, the first of the top three U.S. agricultural counties – which all lie in California – has a take for fruit and produce of over $1 million a day and over $1 billion a year for all agricultural products. California grows 40% of all fruit and nuts in the U.S. and 25% of the vegetables. Production in 1981 totalled 30.4 million tons of field crops, 12 million tons of vegetables and 10.7 million tons of fruit and nuts; the average production values per acre were, respectively, $528, $1,552, and $2,881.

As growing suburbs encroached on farmland, agriculturalists pushed further up the valleys, and roughly a quarter of California land has remained invested in orchards, fields, vineyards, or support of livestock.

Irrigation takes water to more of the land than ever before. Since the time of the Franciscan Fathers, getting a steady supply of water to farmland has been the key to getting a bountiful yield from the fertile soil. They, of course, had built aqueducts and an irrigation system that worked rather well, proving that the land could produce a bounty of goods.

By the 1870s the most desirable acreage, close to streams, had been claimed and with the land went riparian rights. It took court battles and then passage of the so-called Wright Law of 1887 to clear the way for irrigation of more remote areas and formation of irrigation districts. With this new availability of water, previously dry but fertile ground increased in value as much as 40-50 times.

Two Canadians, George and William Chaffey, had a lot to do with improving the irrigation system. They established colonies near San Bernardino (Etiwanda) and Los Angeles (Ontario) and set up mutual stock water companies, selling shares to land buyers. Water from mountain streams was conducted through concrete pipes to each lot. They also developed hydroelectric power plants, using the flow of water to power the first electrically lighted homes in the West. By 1902, George Chaffey had seen to the construction of a canal and over 400 miles of irrigation ditches, taking water from the Colorado River into the desert of southern California, making the soil prosperous.

The main benefit of this wonderful widespread control of the water supply was to citrus growers. Back to the Franciscan missions again: all except three of them had tended fruit orchards, proving California's physical conditions ideal for citrus culture. Then, in the mid-nineteenth century, explorer William Wolfskill started into the business of experimental farming. He took orange trees from the San Gabriel Mission and planted groves that kept multiplying, and he added orchards of lemon trees. The Wolfskill family realized huge profits from the fruit and eventually shipped crates of seedless oranges to the East via transcontinental railroad. Oranges turned up at the Chicago World's Fair sporting labels declaring "I am a Riverside navel orange." Clever marketing of southern California's citrus fruit, especially through co-operatives and associations of growers, kept demand high and created such a boom for growers that by the turn of the century – when the state had become a leading U.S. producer of plums, pears, peaches, cherries, apricots, and apples – the real value was in oranges, lemons, and grapefruit.

More work than just irrigation and good marketing went into the phenomenal success of the citrus industry. The Wolfskill family orchards, again, conducted numerous pioneering experiments in biologically controlling pests, which at times had threatened to wipe out the whole industry. Citrus research stations were established with federal and state governments, and investigators continued to develop pest controls to attack animals and other plants potentially harmful to crops. Some grove owners and botanists perfected varieties of oranges: for example navel oranges, which became the prime winter crop. Engineers invented smokeless heaters to guard against winter freezes. Packing houses sprang up and refrigeration controls improved. All of this activity in California changed the orange from a novelty food to a staple in the American diet, and farm income multiplied many-fold from mid-nineteenth century levels when wheat was the chief crop.

Growers of other commodities also prospered in the twentieth century. Cotton, a latecomer to the state, boomed as the number one crop for a while. The avocado, a subtropical fruit, jumped from obscurity to increasing popularity with U.S. consumers, largely because California growers and marketers promoted its nutritional value, unique texture and flavor. California produces nearly all the almonds grown in the country, which amounts to half the world's supply. The export demand continues to rise. Walnuts, probably originally brought from France, account for most of the national production. These tree crops are harvested by mechanical devices that grab tree limbs and shake nuts to the ground so that sweepers, also mechanized, can pick them up. California's salad bowl crops read like a greengrocer's stock list: apricots, artichokes, asparagus, broccoli, Brussels sprouts, cantaloupes, carrots, cauliflowers, celery, cranshaw melons, garlic, grapes, honeydew melons, kiwi fruit, lima beans, lettuce, mushrooms, olives, onions, peaches, pears, persimmons, plums, spinach, strawberries, sugar beets, tomatoes...

It's not a mom-and-pop roadside stand. It's called agribusiness. The bountiful agricultural wealth did get California comfortably through the Depression, since crops became the chief and most stable economic support for the state. But it hasn't all been peaches-and-cream, so to speak. In the 1960s, Cesar Chavez, probably the best known Mexican-American in the country, started to organize the long-exploited farm workers who were largely unskilled immigrants from Mexico and the Phillipines. Even the U.S. government had been cooperating with the seasonal roundup of cheap foreign labor, although this bracero program officially stopped in 1964. Chavez put together the United Farm Workers Organizing Committee and waged a bitter fight to get higher pay, better conditions and terms for the beleaguered field workers. The grape growers in the San Joaquin Valley incurred a strike, despite the workers' fears of reprisal. The strike continued for several years while growers would hire illegal "wetbacks" to work in the vineyards. Trouble also erupted between Chavez and the Teamsters, who controlled packing labor and were looking to take over field workers. When contracts with UFW would expire, the growers often signed with the older, better-organized Teamsters. Finally, intervention by state government in the form of a farm bill, forced free elections among farm workers so that they could choose which union should represent them in negotiations with growers. All of the strife had attracted national attention, much sympathy and boycotts to support grape and lettuce pickers.

It's as difficult to generalize about California agriculture as it is to generalize about the state itself. Certainly, economic conditions, weather and water, directly affect not only the population of California, but the rest of the country too.

We all eat a lot of what the people of California grow and sell. They eat even more of it. And eating in California is one of the great pleasures of being there. First come the sensuous delights of shopping. Gargantuan supermarkets are numerous in southern California, and many of them stay open 24 hours a day. Home cooks and the best of California's new breed of chefs take their inspiration from the glorious selection and outstanding quality of foods rushed from the farm to their local markets.

These young restaurateurs, caterers, and cooks work as hard and seriously at their craft to turn out sparkling new, innovative dishes, as the farmers do to provide them with the ingredients. Probably the most influential and highly touted restaurant in the U.S. right now belongs to the energetic Alice Waters. Chez Panisse in Berkeley sports a different menu every week. The kitchen demands and gets the best and freshest of the widest selection that California can grow. Cooking style dares to be inventive with classical themes, and the result is a distinctive flair and fine food served with impeccable charm and care.

Entertaining in California has usually meant lots of food, set out buffet fashion for lots of people, often out-of-doors. The trend of centering meals around sports and relaxation, such as tennis, swimming, or jacuzzi, started in southern California. They frequently have just the setting in the backyard: a tennis court, swimming pool, hot tub, or all three. Sunday brunch rituals originated with Californians too.

Now they are claiming responsibility for creating a cuisine that is serious, creative, and influencing the rest of the country. A lot of ideals reflecting California spirit describe this new way of cooking: it uses the best of California's agricultural products. Foods must be healthy and wholesome. Dishes of other cultures – Mexican, Oriental, and French – are adapted and blended with the traditional. Californians are never afraid to try out new things, new foods, or new combinations of foods; and something new is always available. Now there are new melons and new cheeses coming onto the market from California farms. Pioneers of the contemporary cooking world have put all these ideas together with some traditional French techniques.

The new dishes delight the palate with unexpected textures and flavors, and many of them can be characterized as having a light quality. A typical sauce for a simple roast chicken is made with leeks and seedless grapes simmered in white wine; kiwi fruit and grapes in white wine spiced with fresh ginger and soy sauce goes over fish or chicken. Meats, served sparingly, combine with fruits in unlikely ways: lamb cubes with chunks of pineapple and figs in an Oriental sauce; pork and delicate kiwi fruit accented with fresh-squeezed orange juice; homemade sausage prepared with fresh peaches served chilled.

The Chinese in California have always eaten a lot of squab. You can order it prepared Mandarin style in any of San Francisco's Chinatown restaurants, or roast one at home, maybe with a made-from-scratch seasoned stuffing. Korean take-out restaurants have sprung up all over Los Angeles. They prepare braised or barbecued beef ribs in tangy sauces for a low price. The smartest hostesses order up sushi, a fad from Japan. Slender strips of raw fish, exquisitely rolled around pickled rice and wrapped with seaweed, come artistically arranged on a tray. Sushi is exotic, light and oh, so elegant.

California even produces some of its own caviar, and research is going on now at University of California-Davis toward producing more and better sturgeon roe. Meanwhile, the small amounts that are available garnish paste, or get stuffed into vegetables in the restaurants of chefs who snap it up from the market. They would rather serve the native goods than an import.

Fish has become a mainstay of California cooking. The low calorie count and high protein value accounts for the popularity of snapper, sole, halibut, sand dab, cod or salmon fresh from Pacific waters. Piquant sauces with a hint of fruit, or a flavored butter, go nicely with a simple grilled or broiled fillet. Almost any course, especially at an outdoor meal, could include fish or seafood.

The healthy natural food trend probably got started with the hippies. The idea proved to be longer lived than a fad. Californians embrace it as a way of life. Breads are wholewheat; baked at home, or a bakery you can trust for goodness and pure ingredients. Cottage cheese and yogurt dips go with mounds of bite-sized raw veggies at cocktail parties. And then there's the guacamole – puréed avocado made with any of a variety of spices or other vegetables, depending on the tastes of the chef and how experimental he or she wants to be. Californians adopted the basic recipe for this dish from the Mexicans when they transferred the avocado plant to their gardens. Now it's practically a staple in every Californian's diet.

Mexican food – tacos, burritos, enchiladas, chimichangas – in southern California is simple, spicy, hot, and the best you'll find anywhere. Go to restaurants in east Los Angeles or Boyle Heights for the ambiance and plentiful good food. Or try the fast food stands out near Venice. Somehow burritos at the beach always taste best with an orange whip.

The most convenient array of California's fresh and prepared foods is Los Angeles' Farmers Market. This 60-acre complex on Fairfax Avenue near CBS Television City, built during the Depression to give farmers a place to sell their wares, houses just about anything edible: meats, nuts, cheeses, vegetables, fruits, Chinese, Mexican, Italian, Greek, low-cal, junk food, health food, freshly baked breads, elegant pastries. Other specialty shops mix in, and there are lots of nooks and crannies, so be sure you check it out thoroughly. You can dine in one of the restaurants, or get take-out and sit in one of the patio areas where the people-watching is always entertaining.

California's sunlit valleys, from Humbolt County down

to San Diego, host virtually every combination of climate and soil that will nurture grape-bearing vines. The Franciscan Fathers first discovered that conditions were optimal for viticulture, and missions established vineyards, harvested grapes, and made wine for their own religious and social uses. They made brief ventures into commercial production and marketing – the mission in the Sonoma Valley was first – but as a movement, commercial winegrowing began in the early nineteenth century when Joseph Chapman, an American, and Jean Louis Vignes, a Frenchman, in separate operations set out vines in valleys near Los Angeles. With their initial successes, it wasn't long before winegrowing was the principal agricultural industry in the area. Vignes realized that he could produce finer wines with choicer grape varieties; so he sent for European cuttings, planted them, and watched his vineyards flourish. The California wine industry was born.

Agoston Haraszthy, a Hungarian nobleman who had relocated to California for his health, established several vineyards in the San Francisco vicinity in the 1850s, experimenting with different cuttings in various soil and climate variations. He convinced the state government to help him in his research, and Haraszthy, who probably the most to advance viticulture in the state, eventually collected more than 100,000 cuttings of some 300 grape varieties, most of which he planted in the Sonoma Valley. Now the best European varieties were available and flourishing in California. Wine fever replaced the fading gold rush that had changed the state only a decade before.

The fledgling vineyards were all too soon threatened with extinction by *phylloxera*, a dread insect pest which struck Sonoma in 1874. Several years of painstakingly patient scientific experiments proved that *Vitis vinifera* could be grafted onto hardy, native American vine roots, to provide immunity from *phylloxera*. Vineyards in California and Europe were saved from sure destruction.

In the late-nineteenth century, winemaking started the

careers and empire building of dozens of famous and important Californians: George Hearst, William Bowers Bourn, Leland Stanford, James G. Fair, James de Barth Shorb, John A. Stanly, Elias "Luck" Baldwin, and Henry Naglee, among others. They placed their wines on the market throughout the world, too. The transcontinental railroad gave the rest of the country access to native wines, and there are records of shipments to Europe, Canada, Latin America, Australia and the Orient, before 1900. By .1913, 330,000 acres were planted in vineyards, and the wine produced had an annual commercial value of $15 million. Before long, though, one more blow was dealt the industry.

Prohibition came in 1920. Hundreds of wineries closed. Those that survived did so by supplying fresh grapes to amateur winemakers, producing wines for cooking, sacramental or medical purposes which was legal, or by shrinking into little basement wineries and weathering the threat of bankruptcy. With the failure of prohibition and the repeal of the Amendment, increased production from still-existing wineries and vineyards resumed immediately.

California has had a great deal to do with educating Americans in the values and uses of wine. Growers, with the help of the California Department of Agriculture, initiated a marketing campaign in 1938 that included public information and education programs and strengthened advertising. National statistics started to show favorable results: per capita consumption of wine increased steadily, more acres were planted with grapes each year, more wineries opened, and sale of California wines grew annually. Today, California produces over 314 million gallons, more that 85% of all U.S. wines. Grapes, planted on over one half million acres, continue to be the state's most valued food crop.

Some of the best known and loved California wines are the varietals, whose names derive from the grapes grown to make them. U.S. law requires that at least 75% of a bottle comes from the grape variety named on the label. Indulge in a generous sampling of varietal wines to see what a splendid job the growers have done. California Barbera, descendant of growths taken from Italy's Piedmont, yields a dry red wine with a slightly spicy, round, dark taste that balances perfectly with robust California foods. Merlot grapes make a gentle, appealing, new red varietal, and sometimes a little of the juice is blended with the closely related Cabernet Sauvignon to smooth it out. Cabernets, best when aged for a few years, make excellent all-round dinner wines. Gamay, and Gamay Beaujolais, don't come from the same vines, although the light fruity character makes them similar. Gamay or Napa Gamay are actually the true Beaujolais grapes, while a strain of Pinot Noir produces Gamay Beaujolais which should be drunk young. Of all the reds, the smoothest, richest texture belongs to distinctive Pinot Noirs which have been aged properly, usually six to ten years. Californians choose this excellent red wine for special occasions and celebrations. They plant more acres, however, with Zinfandel grapes than any other. It has been called California's mystery grape and produces red wine, with a zingy, berry-like bouquet, that darkens and becomes fuller with age.

White varietal wines from California also come in a fine assortment of characters. Chinon Blanc, similar to its fruity relative from France's Loire Valley, enjoys the widest popularity of all the whites, because the grape can yield wines ranging from dry to quite sweet. Johannisberg Rieslings can vary, too, and if they are sweet and fruity make a delightful drink with dessert. In general, the California whites are fruity wines – even the great tart Chardonnays display at least a slightly fruited bouquet. Try a fume blanc for a dry, fresh, uniquely California varietal wine. It has a pleasant smoky cast and taste.

One of the special treats in present-day California is a trip to wine country. Rather than joining a packaged wine tour (there are several companies offering such services) you should plan your own tour so that your journey can be leisurely and relaxed. In the Napa Valley alone, where there are over 100 wineries, you'll have a choice of almost 50 that have public tours and tastings. Unless you have unlimited time to roam about, select a winery like Domaine Chandon that is unusual and off the well-worn, main tourist trail. I suggest Domaine Chandon because there you will be able to see and learn about traditional oenological methods, cultivation and growing of grapes, production of excellent sparkling wines, and enjoy elegantly prepared California cuisine. It all makes for a festive occasion.

In 1973, Moët & Chandon, for centuries a firm famous for French Champagne, purchased about 1,000 acres in the Napa valley near Yountville, to establish vineyards that could yield comparable, outstanding American products. Located just off Highway 29 and screened from view, San Francisco architects ROMA designed a winery stepped into a hillside, curving along its contour, and blending with the textures of the environment. The walls, built with stones taken from the site, and the wood-beamed ceilings recall historic Napa wineries , and arched roofs and doorways are reminiscent of the caves in France where wine is aged. The carefully judged soil and climate in this part of the Valley proved to be ideal, and the unique French-American association has been successful in creating two excellent sparkling wines: Chandon Napa Valley Brut and Chandon Blanc de Noirs.

Most champagnes are a blend of black and white grapes: the Pinot Noir (black), and Chardonnay and Pinot Blanc (white), combined according to the classic *méthode champenoise*, make Napa Valley Brut. Pinot Noir gives body and aging potential, and Chardonnay adds the acidity necessary for lightness in a well-blended champagne-style cuvée. The oenologist at Domaine Chandon uses 15-30% reserve wines from previous harvests in each year's new cuvée in order to assure continuity of style and quality. Thus you will not find vintage dating on their wines, since U.S. law permits no more that 5% nonvintage wine in a vintage-dated product. Napa Valley Brut is fermented in the bottle, aged "on the yeast", until it is ready for the traditional, laborious process of riddling. This procedure of turning and tilting the bottles of aging wine simply maneuvers

the sediment into position for removal; it is also one of the costliest steps in making sparkling wines. Engineers designed a computerized machine for Domaine Chandon that can riddle 4,032 bottles of wine at once and finish a work cycle in twelve days. Imagine having to complete such a chore by hand! Your hosts will demonstrate the old versus new.

Chandon Blanc de Noirs is blended only from various black grapes, 30% from reserve wines of different harvests. Its glowing "partridge eye" color results from the kind California climate. After grapes have been gently pressed, the oenologist blends the cuvée and, again, it is bottle-aged according to traditional *méthode chapmenoise*. The fruitiness of Pinot Noir balances the brut (dry) finish.

The chef at Domaine Chandon created menus to showcase these two fine wines; some of the dishes are prepared with delicate champagne sauces. Cuisine and service might be described as French relaxed with California setting and style. The elegant surroundings suggest a leisurely lunch which is best enjoyed in two or three courses. You will find fresh fish, seafood, wonderful cheeses and fruits, and a bounty of other California-grown delectables all carefully, exquisitely prepared. For an evening meal you might wish to combine dining with a self-conducted wine tasting. The restaurant's wine list includes an impressive array of Napa Valley wines (mostly still wines) from many outstanding vineyards in the surrounding area.

For a more casual winery tour, take a picnic to Sterling Vineyards, also in the Napa Valley, just south of Calistoga. A tramway will deliver you to the newly constructed Moorish-style winery, where you can move at your own pace through the facilities and then enjoy a generous tasting outdoors on the lawn, or at picnic tables.

Another winery that welcomes picnickers is Buena Vista, one of the oldest vineyards in California, located northeast of the town of Sonoma. Also in the Sonoma Valley, Sebastiani Vineyards offer quite a wide variety of excellent indigenous wines for sampling. The Christian Brothers' Mount La Salle Vineyards in the redwoods north of Napa probably welcomes more visitors to tour its facilities than any winery in the Sonoma or Napa Valleys, and the brothers give an informative historical orientation to the industry. You can visit the novitiate and vineyards and taste a very good selection of wines here.

Don't neglect exploring the quaint little towns in the valleys; Sonoma, Napa, Yountville, St. Helena, Calistoga. They mostly developed in the mid-nineteenth century as adjuncts to the budding wine industry, and to attract tourists to the healthful natural hot springs; and they remain charming respites of Victoriana: Calistoga, whose name was coined by its founder Sam Brannan from "California" and "Saratoga" (famous medicinal springs in New York State), started out as a great resort spa.

The enterprising Brannan made a fortune from the California gold rush: he published the first newspaper in the state, announcing the event; operated the only store in the Sacramento Valley, keeping the miners supplied with food and clothing; and became the state's first banker. Then, with the vision of bringing thousands of tourists and health-seekers to a Mount St. Helena paradise, he overspent on building and maintaining hotels, race tracks, golf courses, and skating rinks, and so lost his millions. The mud and sulphur baths and mineral pools were left behind, and offer today's guests ultimate relaxation and pampering on visits to wine country. Most spas are connected with hotels. Choose from luxurious treatments such as outdoor mineral pools, whirlpools, steam baths, hot mud baths, sulphur steam cabinets, herbal blanket sweats, or massages. Trained personnel at the facilities will assist you.

The movies came to California in 1902, lured by the legend of eternal sunshine. The industry made a lot of people rich and famous, boosted the population and kept tourism and dozens of support industries prospering right through the Depression. The movies quickly became a symbol to the rest of the world of California's cultural achievement. The movies were, in large part, technology and art all wrapped up in a celluloid package and delivered daily to millions of people direct from Hollywood.

So here suddenly developed another West Coast magnet: the talented, schemers, hangers-on, dreamers, and star-struck, descended upon southern California in droves. Mary Pickford, Charlie Chaplin, and Gloria Swanson came to Hollywood and made legend. From its infancy "the industry" made sure the publicity machine kept it enshrouded in myth and image. It paid off. The people who brought their creativity and put it to work in the movies, stood to gain greatly.

In 1923, a talented and determined young dreamer from the Midwest arrived in Hollywood with not much more than an apprenticeship as a cartoonist, a keen eye, and an unwavering desire to work in the movies. A job in someone else's shop did not come easily, so Walt Disney and his brother Roy, who would become his lifelong partner, set up their own. During the next six years he busied himself developing a studio that pioneered new animation techniques and created a character who became virtually a national hero. Mickey Mouse, who has played an important symbolic role in the entertainment industries, not to mention his central place in everyone's childhood, made his auspicious debut from southern California in *Steamboat Willie* under the billing "the first animated cartoon with sound". Mickey Mouse won for himself and his creator, Walt Disney, a special Oscar in 1932. Disney received Academy Awards almost annually after that, and throughout his career he held a strong, almost spiritual, attachment to Mickey.

Walt Disney's success in the entertainment business came directly from his practical philosophy and work method. He let curiosity lead him to discovery and mastered the study of detail. His story and character ideas were frequently derived simply from close, attentive observation, even of ordinary events. Once, he had gone on a camping trip and returned sleepless because sounds of snoring from nearby tents had kept him awake most of the night. He found the incident amusing, repeated the story to his staff writers, and included a snoring scene in *Snow White and the Seven Dwarfs*. Travel became more than just a source of relaxation, information, and inspiration; Disney absorbed new experiences, sights, sounds; and people analyzed them bit by bit until he felt satisfied that he had some new thing to add to his already chockful grab bag of ideas. This unflagging attention to creative detail led him to surround himself with the best talent he could find, and to encourage these young artists and technicians at his studio to pursue their craftsmanship and better their skills. He gave them ideal working conditions: training and direction on-the-job, comfortable surroundings, an ambiance of creative inspiration, and sometimes his own brand of personal avuncular cheerleading. By the time he'd moved his operation to Burbank studios in 1939, the workers labored in conditions of near luxury. Disney's genius was perhaps in expounding his practical theory of seeking an on-the-spot solution to any technical or artistic problem. He would insist that his animators watch live-action film with the sound turned down, so that they could concentrate just on facial movements used in talking and then reproduce what they saw in animated cartoons. Walt Disney was able to realize some of the most remarkable achievements emanating from southern California entertainment resources.

Disney vastly improved the quality of cartoon shorts, added carefully synchronized sound, and, by 1932, perfected the use of color for cartoons. With each new animated series he would take time and care to make sure production included developments of new techniques and themes. By 1934, Disney decided to venture into the feature market with animation. *Snow White and the Seven Dwarfs* required the development of a multiplane camera so that animated characters could appear more life-like and three-dimensional. The test short for the camera was *The Old Mill*, which proved to be an enormous success in its own right. As work continued on the *Snow White* story and characters, Disney "cast" his crew of artists, directors, and cameramen. Each one

was selected to take care of particular details, endowing *Snow White* with qualities of human movement, adding humor and individuality to the dwarfs or setting the background with the air of a fairy tale. Days on end were given to tedious story conferences, preparing one scene at a time and reviewing each for content and technical merit. It all worked beautifully on December 21, 1937 when Walt Disney's shiny new $1.5 million *Snow White and the Seven Dwarfs* premiered at the Carthay Circle Theater in Los Angeles. Hollywood cheered a success that a tenacious genius had produced. Disney sent it out to the rest of the world and grossed eight million dollars.

However, part of his genius was to move right on to other projects and not try to repeat himself. He next chose a more serious subject and a story that included only animal characters – *Bambi*. Here was an even tougher challenge for his animators, since he wanted the deer to look, run, and eat like deer and the rabbits to be rabbits. In typical Disney fashion, he hired a well-known animal painter to lecture the staff on animal structure and movement. At first he brought only a couple of deer to the studio for observation and photographing, but later the menagerie grew to include owls, rabbits, skunks, and other beasts of the outdoors. Stones did not go unturned: Disney made copious notes of his own, remarking on animal traits he wanted replicated on film. Sometimes the daily output dwindled to drawings for less than half a foot of film, rather than the usual ten feet per day. This time, to cope with story problems and to find other solutions that hadn't been forthcoming, Disney assigned key personnel to work exclusively in a special *Bambi* unit. The strategy paid off, at least in one sense. *Bambi*, five years in production, played to throngs around the world and has since become an American cultural classic. Another Disney success, but one that, along with *Pinocchio* and *Fantasia* ate up all the studio's *Snow White* profits.

Money and budgets didn't daunt Walt Disney. Curiosity consumed him, and the quest for perfecting art and the technology needed to make his art come to life, drove him. He also wanted to make people happy with the things he enjoyed. Joel Chandler Harris' 'Uncle Remus' stories had pleased him as a child, so he decided to make them into a feature film. This time, ostensibly to cut costs, he mixed live-action with cartoons. Not only did the inherent problems of combining two film procedures give him a workshop for advancing the medium, but *Song of the South* showed Disney that the time had come to strike out in other directions.

The studio produced what he called "sugar-coated" educational films, realizing that he shouldn't stray too far from pure entertainment. The 'True-Life Adventures' series, with stories built around travel or nature themes, played theaters as features and won Academy Awards as documentaries. *Cinderella*, released in 1950, became the next big animated commercial success. At the same time, he went to work on live-action films, and made an entry into the market with the well-received *Treasure Island*. He also found television, the new entertainment medium that the movie industry viewed as a threat to their business. And shortly after entering the home market, Disney, ever the innovator, and Mickey Mouse, his time-honored symbol of achievement, introduced a new format to the viewing audience – live programming for children. *The Mickey Mouse Club* attracted millions of viewers, attendant merchandising of mouse ears, magazines, phonograph records, and turned a profit for its creators and sponsors.

Television, because of Walt Disney's vision, also made possible one of California's most famous, popular, and enduring entertainment attractions – Disneyland. Once Disney had decided to build an outdoor amusement park, he needed a method to finance his multimillion - dollar dream, and he designed the *Disneyland* series, which by 1955 was the highest-rated show on television, to do just that. In many ways, this many-faceted entertainment project represented the epitome of Walt Disney's creative mind and work process.

He had indulged his fascination with minatures by building the Carolwood-Pacific Railroad along a half mile plot on his Holmby Hills property. It was a scale replica, down to the bunks, washstand, potbellied stove, and newspapers on a rack in the parlor car. Disney decked himself out in an engineer's costume to treat his daughters and friends to rides around the route. For years he'd chosen to study outdoor amusements, observed children and adults at zoos, carnivals, county fairs, and parks all over the world, and concluded that he could create the optimal entertainment form for all ages.

Even the most jaded visitor to Disneyland can find ways to enjoy himself, and then marvel at being taken in by a place jammed with crowds: long waits for rides through manufactured jungles filled with phony mechanical animals or down the silliest little "mountain" that's called, of all things, the Matterhorn; another longer line to get a meal in the restaurant that does not allow alcholic beverages on the premises. You'll have a good time, a very special good time, and you'll wonder how he did it...

How? By the now, well-practiced Disney method of inspiration, study, and quest for all the best answers. He started Disneyland by having the Stanford Research Institute scientifically select a site that could serve year-round. They pinpointed Anaheim, with its almost unvariable, mild climate, near major freeways and what would become the population center of southern California. Disney himself struggled with overall design, which was conceived with a strong sense of continuity throughout the park. He wanted a single entrance so that everyone who entered would start with the same orientation. Visitors should flow comfortably through the park from scene to scene on wide boulevards, or in automatic vehicles. Colors, shapes, and themes would follow patterns of gentle transition, and no one presentation would overwhelm any other, or the visitors themselves. When he needed a certain effect, he would assign an engineer or artist to examine the problems for any and every possible solution. Disney absorbed himself with the project, spending days and nights on end at the site, asking questions interminably, storing in his fertile mind technical information that would lead to more creative development. Disneyland was something completely new, made in his mold from beginning to end. Like everything else the man turned out during his prolific life, it came from his keen perception of the human sense of pleasure and fantasy.

Walk into Disneyland today. You'll find yourself truly transported into another realm. Your eyes will never want for something to do, yet your senses will never feel overwhelmed. Parents don't stand around waiting to shepherd their children from one ride to the next. Disneyland captures the adult imagination and seduces grown-ups into participating with its sophisticated, thoughtful, complex presentation of some very simple concepts – a product and place of such detail and energy that one realizes a stroke of extraordinary genius has been let loose. Genius combined with the ever-present Disney brand of practicality. The immaculate appearance of Disneyland is no accident. A corps of workers assigned just to the garbage detail sees to it that every discarded napkin or soda can is disposed of properly. Chances are you won't crunch on any nutshells on your way to Tomorrowland or Bear Country, as only unshelled nuts are sold in the Main Street shops. Nor will you have to pull the soles of your shoes away from a messy wad of gum, which is also among the merchandise banned from sale in the Kingdom.

As long as he was alive and able, Walt Disney visited his southern California extravaganza almost every day. And not just to escort various heads of state and celebrities. He observed people – their faces, reactions, enjoyment – and dreamed of fresh, new ideas to keep the park vibrant and to improve even on himself.

With all the components that went into his movie, television, and live entertainment production, Walt Disney's main objective was the final visual effect. Music, drawings, acting, technical operations and equipment, all carefully served what the eye absorbed of the final product. His successful results, in large part, came from an obsession to have the best trained

talent contributing to each aspect of the work. Obsession wasn't as far as it went. Disney had always made sure the people at his studio were the most talented and best trained, and after the initial success of Disneyland, he extended his ideals to the formation of the California Institute of the Arts.

Chouinard Art Institute had long been befriended by Disney when, in 1962, he took more active control and merged it with the Los Angeles Conservatory of Music, resulting in CalArts. The Disney way of formally developing young, fertile imaginations went to work again. He wanted to remove restrictions from study in creative fields and allow gifted students active exposure to as many areas and experiences as they could absorb. So he first directed a nationwide study of education in art schools and conservatories; sought advice from leading, innovative educators, and settled on a location north of the San Fernando Valley for the new Institute. Talent will get you into CalArts. Curiosity, diligent work, and artistic expression, all Disney traits, are what he hoped for in a small select student body.

California's two largest cities – Los Angeles and San Francisco – offer the greatest diversity of life styles to be found in any contemporary American urban areas. Popular images of laid-back, freeway, casual, young, and tanned people in the San Fernando Valley, or the Beverly Hills movie stars' posh glamor, describe only part of the population. If you spend any time observing neighborhoods of either city, Californians themselves will change a lot of those preconceived notions you have about them and how they conduct their lives.

Of all cities, Los Angeles is probably the most maligned and San Francisco the most loved. It's almost an American tradition. Easterners who go West feel they could live in San Francisco if they had to. It has a sophisticated, cosmopolitan flair that makes them feel at home right away. Public transportation makes a car unnecessary. The 24-hour, multi-media street life bounces along with a spontaneity and character of its own. Los Angeles, on the other hand, greets the visitor with an unending maze of freeways, overhung with smog. It has no discernible center. Low-lying buildings in lush acres sprawl and sprawl, except for the interruption of mountain ranges dotted with all manner and shapes of houses climbing up and down their faces. The strange spatial arrangements are disconcerting to those who know cities as places of cramped living arrangements, overcrowded subways and buses, teeming sidewalks, and towering skyscrapers.

California cities are popularly thought of as new places. They promote themselves as always being first with the latest, and pop culturalists would agree that most American fads start in California. That's an American tradition, too. But outlandish trends, and being ahead of the times, make up only part of the complex California psyche.

It is not without good reason that trendiness grasps such a hold on the California state of mind. The roots of Los Angeles and San Francisco go back more than two hundred years. But at the time they were founded, each was set up as a small settlement, not a major chunk of modern civilization. Development of these two villages into citie supporting populations of millions came suddenly, swiftly, with little warning or preparation and largely without planning. Leadership and pioneering are intertwined with the respective histories of California's two largest cities.

Los Angeles started life as a sleepy little pueblo, established quite deliberately by the Spanish in 1781, at the urging of the Franciscan Fathers who kept to their own primary concerns of mission work. The area around and about largely supported agriculture. Prosperous rancheros raised livestock, grew olives, oranges, grapes; and the few newcomers, mostly Yankees who drifted in during the next decades, arrived with a restless spirit. Until the 1870s, no one had much use for settling in a town with a reputation for a rough citizenry, spurts of street violence, and vigilantes. It remained a frontier town until the advent of the railroad linking southern California with the transcontinentel line in 1876. Then Los Angeles could

be reached with ease, and word of the natural beauty, in particular the near perfect climate, spread fast. Real estate agents jumped to meet the influx of immigrants and Easterners. The boom enjoyed its day and then life settled back, realizing that here already had sprung up a city to be reckoned with. Still Los Angeles remained cut off on its Pacific side by lack of a good natural harbor.

At the turn of the century there remained only the requirement to select a site for a port – it turned out to be Long Beach on the San Pedro Bay – and to construct it. The other need, a good water supply for an urban populace, came by way of building an aqueduct from the Ownes Valley. The project was enshrouded in controversy, not an unusual circumstance for Los Angeles, but, as hoped, the flow of water persuaded many small communities in the surrounding and outlying areas to join themselves to the city, so that by 1920 it had spread to 360 square miles.

With the stage so perfectly set, the next glistening discovery rounded out the prosperity of southern California: beneath the already valued land of beaches and subdivisions, they struck oil. All that was needed to complete the transformation to a complex manufacturing, industrial and population center, came with World War II. From 1940 to 1950, Los Angeles County doubled in size. Transient servicemen and civilians stayed on to make their homes in southern California. Massive plants opened, and the aviation industry, especially, assumed high levels of production. Some historians wryly note that the War was the biggest thing that ever happened to Los Angeles.

It all continued splendidly into the 1950s and '60s, and without any hesitation the developers, contractors, and real estate agents moved right into the hills, canyons, valleys, and beaches in every direction, filling in all the blanks with housing and people. Not far behind came the inevitable freeways: ubiquitous arteries and symbols of Los Angeles' sprawl.

Living in Los Angeles, especially the towns in the

Valley; Venice, Old Hollywood or Malibu, has the feel of life in the suburbs. Yes, a downtown Los Angeles does exist. But there's never a reason for an Angeleno to go downtown. Whatever they have to do, they hop into their cars to get to it. Never do they walk anywhere. It always seems to be a 30-minute drive to work, shopping, restaurants, the gym, or the beach – all major activities of southern Californians.

The driving, though, focuses the many pictures of the area and puts them into perspective. You get a sense of neighborhoods, a feel for the mosaic – its patterns and colors, a history of these places and how they fit together to make a city.

Out at the beach, an odd little town tucked in between Santa Monica and Marina del Rey currently reigns as the hot spot in which to live, for the 'with it' group, especially transplanted Easterners. Venice thinks of itself as the West Coast's answer to New York's Greenwich Village. First artists and writers found a place to work here, then came the tag-along crowd who brought with them their hip attitudes and roller skates. That's the way to get about Venice these days. Not for serious transportation really, but roller-skating at the beach is just the "in" thing to do.

Only a few short years ago, an unfashionable and unnoticed Venice housed people who couldn't afford more than shabby apartments or run-down bungalows. An overzealous real estate developer at the turn of the century had envisioned a replica of Venice, Italy, with houses situated on a network of canals, so that residents could enjoy an enlightened splendor and elegance right on the Pacific. Since tidal action didn't serve well enough to keep the canals clear the outlandish idea was doomed to failure, and Venice went bankrupt. It slid into the businesses of sideshows and weekend amusement parks and nests of run-down buildings for transients. Today, after some renovating, Venice flourishes in ways its original planner wouldn't believe. The galleries, delis, shops, restaurants, and well-kept, quiet little streets away from the beachfront offer neighborhood pleasantries at an unassuming pace.

Blocks of seedy stucco bungalows, still faint with pride of better years, sit humbly by palm trees on the streets of old Hollywood. They housed workers in the early days of movie making, and you pass other reminders of those times – faded film palaces, Paramount Studios on Melrose Avenue, even the restored Hollywood sign marching across the hills above. More of "the industry" still thrives than meets the casual eye. Restaurants on some of the busier boulevards (Highland, La Cienega, Melrose, Sunset) buzz with lunchtime crowds of agents and clients, young actors waiting for a call back that could be their break, and record company executives. Further east, on Vermont Avenue, just on the edges of the comfortable Los Feliz community, step into Chatterton's bookstore late of an evening, where you are welcome to browse away some hours. Settle back in a well-worn armchair or pick through bargains among publishers' remainders. The store stocks an amazing and thorough selection of books in many fields; the staff are knowledgeable and courteous, and if they don't have a title they'll try to order it for you. They also choose the most wonderful music to enhance your browsing pleasure.

In the nearby Wilshire District, where larger homes command lawns that are lush and shady, you will find some fine buildings of Art Deco design and gracious wrought-iron lampposts set out on grassy strips dividing wide residential boulevards. Art Deco really came into its own expression in Los Angeles, and many of these buildings from the 1930s remain. Look for that blocked - out angular line with symbolic decoration. Bullock's Wilshire department store near Douglas McArthur Park is a masterful example and has been designated a historical cultural landmark.

For newer charm, drive up to Mulholland Drive, which runs along the crest of the hills, and around in the hills between the Los Angeles and San Fernando Valleys. You will start to see how California seduced millions into giving up stuffy city life. Streets wind around the scruffy terrain. Houses blend with their settings, surrounded by careful landscaping; or they jut defiantly, sometimes on stilts, from the steep hillsides. Not one misses the opportunity of views for miles. At night, the valleys below drift like a dazzling carpet of light.

One of the older hill districts – the choice neighborhood of film and television set designers, camera people, and other creative types – Silver Lake rises abruptly from Sunset Boulevard and overlooks the downtown Los Angeles area. A parade of immaculate, neat, individualistic homes bends around quick curves. The compact area retains its own special ambiance and seclusion.

A 1920s real estate development that hasn't lost its appeal to the more moneyed "industry" people still retains the status of being an incorporated city within a city: Los Angeles surrounds Beverly Hills, which started out as desert land and grew to be a posh, exclusive, and expensive community. To live there you need maids, gardeners, a pool man, and a lot of money. To live in Bel Air, the adjacent neighborhood, you have to have even more money. Houses start selling at around $1 million. Guarded gates offer, symbolically at least, protection from the rest of the world. The other gated, moneyed community is Malibu, a residential beach strip several miles north of Santa Monica.

Neighborhood flavor and personality come from the attitudes of the residents. On the whole, southern California life centers around the home. Emphasis goes beyond installation of pools and tennis courts on residential property which is, by now, commonplace. Potters work at home on wheels installed out-of-doors lest they miss a ray of sunshine. Lavish entertainment can be put together at the last minute – everything's on wheels here – caterers, musicians, hairdressers and servants respond to house calls. Angelenos move to the beach so that waves and surf will be a part of their domicile. They take pride in homes that are more than just a roof over their heads.

Likewise San Franciscans. But their pride is tinged with some reserve. They are not quite so laid-back. And their neighborhoods are smaller. And they won't necessarily run errands by car.

Their city got its start at about the same time Los Angeles did. The Bay had been discovered and explored as early as 1542, but not until the Franciscans established a mission and presidio in 1776 did Spanish settlers come to live in the area. The Russians built themselves a base for fur trading 100 miles north of the Bay, yet natural resources of the region did not attract other pioneers until the 1820s and '30s. By then the adventurous spirit found in Americans had led them Westward little by little.

It took the discovery of gold to bring them in great numbers, though. Foreigners came, too, with their own dreams. These thousands, their fortunes and disappointments changed the face of the city on the Bay. The international composition of the populace, the great wealth which poured out of the mines, and the opening up of transportation by land and sea, all helped form the present day character of San Francisco.

Of course, much of what was nineteenth century San Francisco didn't survive the 1906 earthquake and fire. But you can still enjoy enough of the historical flair. Rows of Victorian gingerbread houses that have been lovingly cared for climb the steep streets. Some of these bay-windowed charmers have been turned into luxurious bed & breakfast inns that welcome guests into the style and comfort of another era.

The cable cars – universal symbol of San Francisco – climb the hills as they first did over 100 years ago. Andrew Hallidie owned a company that produced wire, rope and cable for the mines in the Sierra Nevada, and he put these materials together and invented conveyances for the city. The system opened in 1873 and, except for a few years off for repairs and maintenance, has operated ever since.

But don't miss San Francisco's newest way to get about:

BART (Bay Area Rapid Transit). The sophisticated, often cranky, computerized rapid rail lines whisk commuters under the Bay to Oakland and communities beyond. The trains will take you out to Berkeley, home of the University of California, one of the country's leading universities and research centers and scene of numerous student uprisings and demonstrations in the 1960s.

San Francisco's other transportation landmark, the Golden Gate Bridge, stands as a beautiful man-made suspension of steel and concrete built in the 1930s, giving thousands of workers and visitors from the northern counties easy entry to California's second largest city.

Transportation, or the making of it, played a curious role in developing ethnic patterns. Huge numbers of Chinese arrived from the Far East at the time of the gold rush, because economic opportunities seemed brighter in the new world than some of the war torn provinces. The first Chinese laundry in San Francisco opened in 1850 and, within 20 years, 2,000 such establishments had sprung up. The builders of the great railroads soon realized the advantages of cheap, imported labor and brought even more Chinese into the Bay area. Almost 15,000 of them toiled for small wages to complete the Union Pacific line. They met with scorn and animosity from unskilled white workers with whom they were competing for employment. Even Congress dealt severely with the new Americans from the Orient. The influx of immigrants was temporarily halted by law, and some Chinese were expelled from the country. The strife of decades that followed, commonly referred to as tong wars, took place in struggles for leadership within the community. Then the events of 1906 pulled everyone together to reconstruct a largely demolished San Francisco.

Chinatown today, bright and festive and full of Oriental smells, sights and sounds, occupies an area between Nob Hill, Union Square, the Financial District, and Telegraph Hill. A huge Oriental arch on Grant Avenue sets off this homogenous neighborhood. It

teems with life 24 hours a day, welcoming visitors to its restaurants, shops, and celebrations. Try to be there for Chinese New Year which takes place between January 20 and February 20 every year. Firecrackers rip through the air and the rowdiness begins. It lasts for two weeks, culminating in a fanciful costume parade looping all through the city, to the accompaniment of gongs, drums, flares, and bands. The star attraction has 50 pairs of legs to support its 150 foot long body – the dragon which winds and twists and shakes all along the parade route.

San Francisco's street life provides year-round entertainment. Some of the talent actually earns a living from sidewalk antics. Around Union Square you are likely to encounter musicians: usually small ensembles from the imaginative banjo band, the San Francisco Medicine Ball; to student brass quintets; to groups playing early chamber music on original instruments. Don't miss the mimes and clowns. Frequently they perform on the waterfront near picturesque Fisherman's Wharf or Ghirardelli Square where lots of tourists usually throng. And is there another city whose sidewalks boast a human jukebox?

If you prefer more formal cultural presentations, the theater district is nearby (Geary Street and thereabouts), usually with some Broadway imports and productions of its own. American Conservatory Theater is the oldest regional theater in the U.S. and one of the most highly regarded. They run a season of seven plays. San Francisco has an opera company and ballet and modern dance troupes. The M. H. de Young Memorial Museum exhibits one of the most outstanding and diversified collections of European and American art in the West. It also houses a special collection of art and artifacts relating the history of California.

Enjoy formality out-of-doors at the Japanese Tea Garden in Golden Gate Park. It's been here since its careful creation in 1894. Bridges lead over tranquil ponds, past pagodas and bonsai, to an authentic Oriental tea house. To experience nineteenth-century Western opulence, go to the Palace Hotel for brunch where a covered courtyard hung with grandiose chandeliers and filled with great pots of greenery and trees reaching toward the canopy of filtering sunlight, gives this gracious room an elegant glow. The original hotel, felled by the quake, was built to be the grandest ever and served as a model for the present structure.

Victorian elegance of the most extravagant expression is shown off on Nob Hill. The railroad barons and millionaire miners tried to one-up each other when they built mansions in this still exclusive neighborhood. Only one of them remains standing; it belonged to mine owner James Flood and now houses the Pacific Union Club. The streets are quiet now, and even the park speaks serenely of the uppercrust who make their homes in this privileged enclave. More of the elite reside in the discreet but ritzy Pacific Heights area. The houses enjoy superb views of the Bay, while manicured shrubbery cuts them off from the ordinary world. Privacy is a cherished commodity in San Francisco neighborhoods.

Mingle a little with the literati at City Lights Bookstore. The Beats of the 1950s headquartered themselves here and it has remained a central focus for the city's progressive thinkers and intellectual activists. Founded in 1953 by poet Lawrence Ferlinghetti, it was the first U.S. bookstore to specialize exclusively in paperback books. City Lights has fostered the careers of many struggling West Coast poets, and sometimes issues their works under its own imprint. Customers linger to browse the shelves and are welcome to sit and read for hours. It's San Francisco tradition and hospitality.

Across the Bridge in Marin County the life style changes – the people are laid-back; they just cool out when things get too far-out. Well, the language changes, but maybe you can relate to it.

The line fuzzes sometimes – what's the truth of California and when, how, why does it become myth? California seems to work or play very hard at being first, or most, or hippest, or richest, or weirdest or glitziest, but always larger than real life.

Right now, its more than 23 million residents make it the most populated state in the U.S. California also has more divorces, pets, cars, miles of freeway, National Parks, business bankruptcies, public beaches and bank robberies, than any other state. California leads the U.S. in gold production, the aerospace industry, and cigarette consumption. It leads the world in motion picture production, has the world's largest city by land area (Los Angeles), the world's largest landlocked harbor (San Francisco), and busiest freeway interchange (downtown Los Angeles where the Harbor, Pasadena, Santa Ana, and San Bernardino Freeways intersect).

Californians spend more on recreation and sports, and have more places to enjoy leisure, than anyone else. Marina del Rey is the largest pleasure boat marina in the world. More professional athletes make their home in California than in any other state. They've assembled the world's largest collection of wild animals at the San Diego Zoo. And Californians have more backyard swimming pools than any other Americans. They'll tell you, too, that they go to bed earlier and get up earlier than the rest of us, just to enjoy all of this pleasure and then work harder to earn even more money to build and buy the next greater pleasure.

San Francisco contains the largest Oriental community outside the Far East. It's also the national capital for suicide and alcoholism. No other state has two major symphony orchestras. San Francisco and Los Angeles each have regional theaters – American Conservatory Theater and The Mark Taper Forum – that have both the largest budgets, and audiences, in the country.

Californians claim an assortment of strange facts. They host the world's lowest golf tournament, played 178 feet below sea level, at Furnace creek in Death Valley. To get up and down one of its hills, San Francisco built the world's crookedest street. They live in a phenomenal state and do phenomenal things there.

Many of the greatest fortunes ever accumulated came as a result of the discovery, by John Marshal, of gold in the California hills in 1848. No other event in California history changed so many lives, or so influenced the shape of destiny for the state. The myth had persisted for centuries that California held the elusive El Dorado with its inestimable powers to change human experience. When the quest became a sudden reality, the frontier of an unprepared California opened up to the world.

Gold, or the discovery of it, has always captured the imagination as no other fantasy has; and when word reached San Francisco that this powerful, mystical element lay less than 100 miles away in the Sierra foothills, the hundreds of that city's inhabitants exited, leaving only seven behind. People from every state in the Union joined the scramble. One hundred thousand of them came from all parts of the world by 1850, traveling the treacherous overland route; or by steamship around Cape Horn, or from Panama's isthmus in overcrowded conditions that bred disease. Entire families invested their life savings in a Westward journey on a chance to know wealth untold.

The events of the gold rush, one-by-one, comprise an astonishing chronicle of California history. The results of all that occurred in 1848, and the following decades, confirms the state's image as the land of ultimate opportunity. John Sutter, Marshall's associate, quickly negotiated land rights from the Indians in the valley where he had his fort, for $200. That action was just about meaningless and served as no deterrent at all: gold seekers came pouring in from everywhere, as soon as they had seen the evidential nuggets and vials of gold dust. Individual tales of California fortune can still stun the imagination. They say it was possible for one person to accumulate $75,000 in just a few weeks of digging, or easily pick up $1,000 a day for not much hunting at all. A child found a single nugget weighing nearly seven pounds. Some nuggets exceeded 20 pounds, and gold dust went for $18 an ounce. Four miners took a six by ten foot claim area, and in eleven days dug $13,750 worth of gold. Men commonly walked around mining camps with thousands of dollars in their pockets.

Gold seeking at first was quite an individual effort, each man setting out, journeying, arriving on his own, and then panning for himself. Later, the more enterprising or greedy of the early arrivers realized their findings and wealth could be multiplied by forcing gold from the earth. And with the opening of the mines, especially hydraulic mines, as much as $50,000 a day in gold could be taken. But the men who ended up laboring in the mines, with no share in the profits, earned sometimes as little as a paltry $4 for a grueling day's work. Rewards from nature and man were less than fair.

And the costs of living, in this greatest of all California adventures, didn't exactly take an even toll. Much of the new wealth had to be spent before it could be enjoyed. Just the necessities of life, precious commodities in this unsettled land lacking in every human convenience, cost dearly. Flour went for $1 a pound. One egg could be astronomically valued at as much as $3! Dried beef or bacon cost $2 a pound; whiskey, $16 a fifth. Newspapers from back East were worth anywhere from $1 to $5. If you had to see a doctor – and the hardships of long travel plus primitive conditions at the mine sites bred disease and ill health – chances are he earned about $100 a day, if you could get an appointment at all. One ambitious young woman charged miners a total of $11,000 for pies made in her single skillet.

The gold rush caught California by surprise, with no time to prepare for the great population boom. Services and service personnel were at a bare minimum. Ships carried laundry to as far away as Hawaii and returned with more anxious gold seekers. 'Gold fever', which aptly describes the mania, spread around the world. Word traveled fast, usually exaggerating the possibilities for great personal gain. The myth even persisted that all this gold came from some single source, high and faraway in the niches of the Sierra, and that only surface particles had washed down to the foothills. The most believing of the fortune-seekers set out to search for this never-found mother lode.

The most secure reward came to those who stayed behind. They assumed the seemingly unexciting tasks of traders, merchants, blacksmiths, manufacturers, shippers, bankers – providing all the goods and services the newly arrived population needed for everyday life and everything the miners needed in the fields and at campsites. San Francisco particularly had never dreamt of such growth in size or importance, nor that it would so suddenly be thrust into a position of international prominence as a commercial, trading and banking center. By 1855, the city published more newspapers (a total of 91, in French, German, Spanish, Chinese and other languages) than did London, and more books than were published in the rest of the U.S. Two telegraph lines linked California with the rest of the world. And just to keep themselves going, Californians had constructed a sugar refinery, 4 distilleries, 18 tanneries, a paper mill, 373 saw mills, and 131 grist mills, in addition to foundries and machine shops. All of this was accomplished by the mid-1850s. The gold boom had a shorter life span than is popularly believed. By 1860, California's annual manufacturing grosses exceeded gold production values.

In 1850, dry goods dealer Levi Strauss arrived in San Francisco from Bavaria, after a sojourn in New York. He packed up bolts of heavy fabric, threads, and needles and headed West, thinking he would outfit the field miners with durable tents. Instead he found the miners more in need of clothing than ready-made shelter, so he designed heavy duty work trousers, reinforced for long wear with small metal rivets. The enterprise he started grew to international proportions and is still around today. So are the pants he designed. Italian Domingo Ghirardelli, whose renovated factory buildings attract today's tourists to their clever shops and restaurants, turned up in San Francisco with his mysterious Guatemalan discovery – chocolate – and built a huge food processing and trade business. Originally he intended to sell to newly prospering miners, but as the commodities supply grew to include coffee, spices, and mustard, Ghirardelli became an international trader.

Many famous San Franciscans, whose names are immortalized today, made their first great fortunes from merchandising and industry that surrounded the gold rush. Leland Stanford, Collis P. Huntington, Charles Crocker, and Mark Hopkins, all originally built small retailing businesses that turned nice profits. Then they really cashed in. Working together unscrupulously to wheel and deal, they manipulated their way to Washington and control of the Central Pacific Railroad. With federal money and transcontinental rights in their authority, these men saw to it that the transcontinental railroad became reality. Now they owned transport for their goods to any point in the U.S. They continued to buy up local rail lines, eventually acquiring exclusive access to all California inland and water transport around the San Francisco Bay area. This created a monopoly so powerful that it took a Federal Act, in 1913, to break it up. But by this time each of the Big Four, as these men were known collectively, had become a millionaire many times over.

One young man from Missouri who set out to seek his fortune in California'a gold rush, actually found it as a miner. George Hearst eventually put together an estate that, when he died in 1891, was estimated at $18 million. He started humbly in the gold fields and tenaciously made his way, right to the U.S. Senate. His son, William Randolph Hearst, stood to gain much of the wealth but went on his own spectacular career as well. Since college days he had wanted to be a journalist, so he set up a California newspaper publishing business that grew into a gigantic concern and made him one of America's richest men.

His fortune secured, William Randolph Hearst decided to celebrate it by building the estate of his, or anybody else's, fantasy. He inherited land at San Simeon that his father had bought with some of his gold fortune for 70c an acre, and in 1919 started to put together the ultimate playground on this 270,000 acre ranch. Two thousand acres were fenced off for a private zoo, stocked with zebras, lions, elk, Barbary sheep, polar bears, fallow deer, cheetahs, fahr goats, and other exotica. Twenty gardeners sowed hillsides with wild flowers to add color to the vistas. The landscaped hills alone cost $1 million.

On a central hill, rising 2,000 feet, Hearst chose to situate a massive 100-room (including 38 bathrooms!) white-marble mansion that, on the exterior at least, resembles a Spanish alcazar. The design was given over to no one architect, although credit sometimes goes to Julia Morgan. Instead, Hearst liked to supervise work on the 32-year project (still not completed when he died in 1951) himself, using a group of recent architecture school graduates. At one point he wasn't satisfied with the towers, they were too simple, so he had them torn away and more ornate designs substituted.

Often his architects would go abroad to acquire various works of art, or to purchase and disassemble palaces or parts of them, to be used in the San Simeon castle. The vast collections of art and architecture – Hearst traveled a great deal himself, always returning with massive and valuable treasures – would be shipped by steamer to the little fishing village of San Simeon that had never in all its days seen quite such activity. Some of the art never made it to the estate and is still stored in warehouses.

So the design of La Casa Grande grew around the walls, ceilings, floors, and rooms of various styles and eras: Medieval, Renaissance, Baroque, Moorish, Greco-Roman, Hispano, Florentine, Persian, and others. One floor is a Pompeiian mosaic from 60 B.C. In addition, he constructed three nearby guest houses, modeled after French chateaux, with 46 rooms. Hearst frequently had guests driven or flown to this playground. It has its own airfield, of course. Eighty of them could sit down to dinner at once in the formal dining room and then retire to a fully equipped theatre for a special screening. However, guests were not permitted liquor in any of the 31 bedrooms. Nor should anyone there ever mention the word "death".

Today, more visitors than ever traipse to Hearst's Pacific paradise. His family couldn't afford the upkeep and gave the estate to the state of California in 1952.

They have opened it to the public. The buildings and properties, with fabulous fountains, pools, and formal Italian gardens, are so vast that you have to select from three different tours, each lasting two hours. All the land you can view from the castle belonged to William Randolph Hearst. This fanciful California dwelling sits majestically, 43 miles north of San Luis Obispo, drenched by coastal sunshine.

Experience your own fantasies in California. Do the ultimate shopping spree in Beverly Hills on Rodeo Drive. The shops here and their wares are as flamboyant as Hearst ever dreamed. These few blocks between Wilshire and Little Santa Monica Boulevards may be the most expensive and desirable pieces of real estate in the world. At least for now, Rodeo Drive is unashamedly faddish, and what's hot today could be as passé as hula hoops by tomorrow. Your car will be parked by valet at the store of your choice, unless you come in a Rolls-Royce, which can be left right outside for an extra tip. Inside the shops, where shoppers select $95,000 chinchilla bedspreads, gold leather shorts, and mother-of-pearl inlaid revolvers, the cordial sales clerks offer white wine or espresso. While you make up your mind whether to take home a cashmere coat lined in mink for $7,500, or just run into Georgette Klinger for a facial, you can shoot a game of pool.

Play your game and eat it too – chocolate Monopoly sets go for $600. It's retailing on a sybaritic glitz binge: gold lamé nightgowns, black leather boxer shorts, silks, imported woolens. Actually, some very fine European and American designers have opened businesses on Rodeo Drive, and you can shop seriously for choice antiques if your bank account is the right size.

You might as well enjoy the natives in their fantastic madness. They have learned to make fun of themselves. "The Beverly Hills Game of Wealth and Status", is a Rodeo Drive best seller at $30. The object is to gain maximum status by going to the right places and saying the right things, while earning lots and lots of money. If you fail to achieve these dual goals you must move to the San Fernando Valley.

Since the time of the earliest California settlers, people have been writing about California and California experiences. Some of the observers kept detailed journals of their activities as they made difficult journeys, or established new settlements in a foreign land, or pioneered in strange, uncharted endeavors, or took up an unfamiliar occupation. The natural beauty inspired others to describe California poetically, or to choose California settings, characters, and stories for their novels.

Writers turned to social comment about the people of the state, their communities, and historical events. Literary expression empowered causes and movements to save California wild life for posterity, or advance a human rights effort. Humorists made Californians laugh at themselves. Literary artists romanticized California as the home of the American dream.

Padre Junipero Serra, the diligent soul and progressive thinker, who labored to build his chain of missions and open up this vast land of contrast, recorded his day-by-day activities from the time of his arrival at San Diego in 1769. In setting out to select a site, for what was to be the seventh of the nine missions which he personally established, he made these notes on the lay of the land: "In the lower part of a green and leafy plain … there are fine stretches of land, abundant feed, much water and trees everywhere, and from an enormous lake right in the middle a canal flows to the ocean. You can see the ocean through an opening between the hills in front … A good deal of the ground is covered with rushes and tule reeds, and among the willows you see quantities of grapevines. On the north side is the beginning of a canyon which branches off according to the twists in the mountain range. It is choke-full of massive trees with enormous branches. We all agreed that it was a wonderful location for another mission. I called it San Juan de Capistrano." The mission was dedicated on the land in 1776.

The greatest explorer and recorder in all California annals, naturalist John Muir, wrote volumes about the flora and fauna and geophysics of his beloved Sierra Nevada. He took down details of nature with his keen senses and turned days of research into poetry. Once, in the upper Yosémite, he watched the sky and described what he saw: "During two whole days of storm … the clouds … were inspired with corresponding activity and life. Clouds rose hastily, upon some errand, to the very summit of the (canyon) walls, with a single effort, and as suddenly returned; or, sweeping horizontally, near the ground, draggled long-bent streamers through the pine-tops; while others traveled up and down Indian Canyon, and overtopped the highest brows, then suddenly drooped and condensed, or, thinning to gauze, veiled half the valley, leaving here and there a summit looming along. These clouds, and the crooked cascades, raised the valley-rocks to double their height, for the eye, mounting from cloud to cloud, and from angle to angle upon the cascades, obtained a truer measure of their sublime stature." A cascade Muir endowed with celestial characteristics: he claimed that the water was "glancing this way and that, filled with bounce and dance and joyous hurrah, yet earnest as tempest, and singing like angels loose on a frolic from heaven." California nature gave him his "visions and dreams" in such abundance that they proved "too many for ink and narrow paper."

Poet Robinson Jeffers, probably the most enamored of all writers on the subject, spent many of his working days where he set most all his writing; in the country by the coast near Carmel. In *Carmel Point:*

"Unbroken field of poppy and lupin walled with clean cliffs;
No intrusion but two or three horses pasturing,

Or a few milch cows rubbing their flanks on the outcrop rockheads…"now, "defaced with a crop of suburban houses…"

Jeffers even drew the California oceanside in his characters; they express themselves in terms of the sea, and have dreams and visions of the Pacific. And, again in poetry, from *Ocean,* pictures creatures of the ocean:

"The gray whales are going south: I see their fountains
Rise from the black sea: great dark bulks of hot blood
Plowing the deep cold sea to their trysting-place".
Writers came Westward, or watched the thousands of others who journeyed to seek California promise of wealth and goodness. Henry David Thoreau found it disconcerting: "The rush to California... reflects the greatest disgrace on mankind. That so many are ready to live by luck and so get the means of commanding the labor of others less lucky, without contributing any value to society – and that's called enterprise!"

Robert Louis Stevenson, as the transcontinental train carried people closer to the Pacific terminus, commented: "All the passengers...thronged with shining eyes upon the platform...At every turn we could look further into the land of our happy future. At every turn the cocks were tossing their clear notes into the golden air and crowing for the new day and new country. For this indeed was 'the good country' we have been going to so long."

And after they had been in the good, new promised land of California, writers and journalists took on a variety of opinions.

Bret Harte on San Francisco: "serene, indifferent of fate."

Rudyard Kipling: "San Francisco has only one drawback – 'tis hard to leave."

William Saroyan: "If you're alive, you can't be bored in San Francisco."

Will Rogers: "Cities are like gentlemen, they are born, not made. You are either a city, or you are not. I bet San Francisco was a city from the very first time it had a dozen settlers!"

Mark Twain (on the Sierra Nevada): "The air up there...is very pure and fine, bracing and delicious. And why shouldn't it be? – it is the same air the angels breathe."

Jack London (of Mount Shasta): "A moving picture in the sky."

O. Henry: "Californians are a rare breed of people, they are not merely inhabitants of a state."

John Gunther: "California is stuck with so many crackpots because they can't go any further."

But whoever you agree with, the fact remains that California is a magical state, which will draw you in and envelop you with its glorious qualities and wonderful way of life.

Previous page: golden California, land of sunshine, mists and rolling hills. It is also a land of rich diversity. *Left* Sherman Gilbert House, San Diego Old Town, with similarly styled buildings *below.* In Balboa Park *bottom left* and the Coronado Hotel *bottom right. Opposite page:* the *Star of India* rests in San Diego harbor.

This page: left the Charthouse Golf Course and the graceful sweep of the San Diego-Coronado Bay Bridge. Below left many of the old adobe buildings in the Old Town have been converted from their original use as part of Mission San Diego de Alcala, into quaint restaurants and shops. Below known as the 'Mother of Missions', Mission San Diego was founded by Padre Juniper Serra and stands serenely in the sunshine.
Opposite page: left La Jolla, north of San Diego, enjoys all the benefits of sun, sand and sea. Here is also the Scripps Institution of Oceanography and the Salk Institute for Biological Studies. Just off the coast lies an extensively studied submarine canyon, known as Scripps Canyon. Top right the California Tower in Balboa Park. Center right the fine and historic Hotel Del Coronado. Bottom right the old lighthouse was erected on top of Point Loma in 1855. However, because its light was often obscured by cloud, the present Coast Guard Lighthouse was built, in 1891, close to the water's edge.

The storm clouds *above* may seem threatening, but they hold
the promise of rain for the Anza-Borrego Desert State
Park. The multifarious cacti *opposite page* inhabit the
Living Desert Reserve, which is a 360-acre area in Palm
Desert, about 15 miles southeast of Palm Springs.

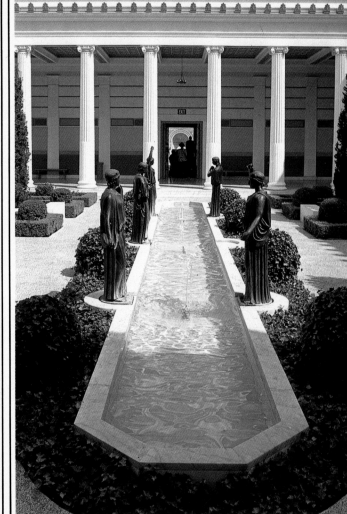

Opposite page: left the winding magnificence of the stairway at Mission Inn. The building is rightly recognized as one of the most beautiful in California, although its origins are as a humble adobe cottage begun in 1875. *Top right* the fourth mission to be dedicated in California was Mission San Gabriel with its cool, vaulted cloisters. *Bottom right* Santa Barbara Court House resembles a Spanish-Moorish castle.
This page: top left the cool, landscaped features of the Walter Annenberg Estate, Palm Springs. *Left and above* the J. Paul Getty Museum has been set out in the style of the Villa dei Papiri, which was sited in the ancient city of Herculaneum, near Pompeii, extant around the 1st century. The Museum building contains marble and bronze sculptures, mosaics and vases, with a wide selection of Western pictorial art.

Described as "the eighth engineering masterpiece of the world", the Palm Springs tramway *left* rises high into the mountains of San Jacinto. Bob Hope has made his home *below* on one of the mountain plateaus in this isolated region, enjoying magnificent views from this lofty perch.

Los Angeles, 'The Big Orange', sprawls to the northwards over the mountains of Santa Monica and south towards the Pacific. Intricate freeways link the scattered metropolis and bright lights light up the night *right* in this city of the car. *Left* Western Avenue and *far left* the City Hall, once the tallest building in Southern California. For those people who wish to escape the city life, however, there are lovely coastal resorts *above and top left* where Pacific surf and the shade of palm trees brings a sense of peace.

Los Angeles takes on an oriental aspect in its Chinatown *these pages*, where the images suggested by the pagoda-styled buildings are compounded by the pungence of aromatic spices and incense. Here you can indulge yourself with delicious Chinese cuisine or just meander through the bustling streets. Sited on Hollywood Boulevard is Mann's Chinese Theater *opposite page, bottom right*, where the footprints, handprints and signatures of the movie stars are immortalized in concrete.

Los Angeles displays many fine new buildings in its city center. *Left* the Union Bank Building and the Bonaventure Hotel. The magnificent Dorothy Chandler Pavilion *below* and the Mark Taper Forum *bottom left,* together with the Ahmanson Theater, form the Los Angeles Music Center for the Performing Arts. The Century Plaza and Schubert Theater *bottom right.* Traffic flows along the Harbor Freeway *opposite page* in the Downtown area.

In the Botanical Gardens at Huntington *left* there is an immense variety of cacti and other flora to be seen. The favorable climate ensures the presence of the ubiquitous palm trees *below* lining the streets. *Bottom* situated in San Pedro along the main channel of Los Angeles Harbor, Ports O'Call and Whaler's Wharf recapture the atmosphere of New England seacoast villages. Colonial style shops and restaurants, with their quaint, tavern-like signs outside, line the cobbled streets.

Opposite page: Pasadena is well-known for its Rose Bowl Stadium where, on New Year's Day, football fans fill the arena to watch this classic championship match. *Top left* the City Hall, in all its ornate glory, reflects the Spanish inspired architecture which was popular in the 1920s. *Remaining photographs* Los Angeles is justly famous for its racing parks, such as Santa Anita Park and Hollywood Park Racetrack, many containing magnificent tropical gardens and elegant restaurants as well as some of the world's top racehorses on the flat, or trotting *bottom right* in lightweight two-wheeled sulkies.

Bonaventure Hotel *below*. Wonderful, wealthy Beverly Hills with its lush Plaza *left*. The palatial Hotel Beverly Wilshire *opposite page*. The 207-acre Huntingdon estate *bottom right* contains a well-planned Botanical Gardens and the Library and Art Gallery building. The Court House in Santa Barbara *bottom left* reflects images of 'Old Spain'.

The Hollywood and the Movieland Wax Museum enshrine the greatest movie stars: *left* Yul Brynner and Deborah Kerr in 'The King and I'; *bottom left* Mae West; *bottom center* Marilyn Monroe in 'The Seven-Year Itch' and *below* Elvis Presley. *Opposite page: top left* John Wayne in 'Hondo'; *top right* Fred Astaire and Ginger Rogers in 'Top Hat'; *bottom left* Julie Andrews in 'Mary Poppins' and *bottom right* Charlie Chaplin in 'The Gold Rush'.

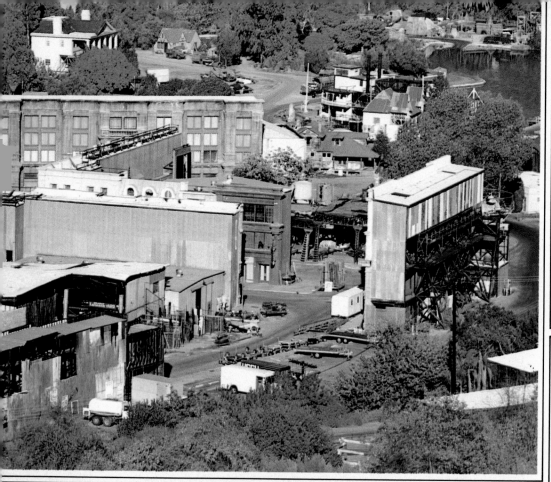

Universal City Studios *this page* is the largest motion-picture studio in the world, covering more than 420 acres. Two and a half million visitors come to Universal each year and conducted tours are provided. There are many different sets to be seen, from the Wild West where stuntmen show their skills *above and top right*, to the ferocious shark *right* in 'Jaws'. *Opposite page:* after 31 years of Atlantic crossings, the *Queen Mary* now rests at Long Beach. The stately liner's attractions include shops, restaurants and the world's largest marine exhibition.

This page: harbor fishing boats, yachts and tuna clippers crowd Ports O'Call and Whaler's Wharf. *Above and right* ever-popular skateboarding. Los Angeles, sunny pleasure land of the West, is full of possibilities for the young at heart. Newport Beach and Balboa is 35 miles south of Los Angeles, attracting fishermen *opposite page, bottom right* to its shores.

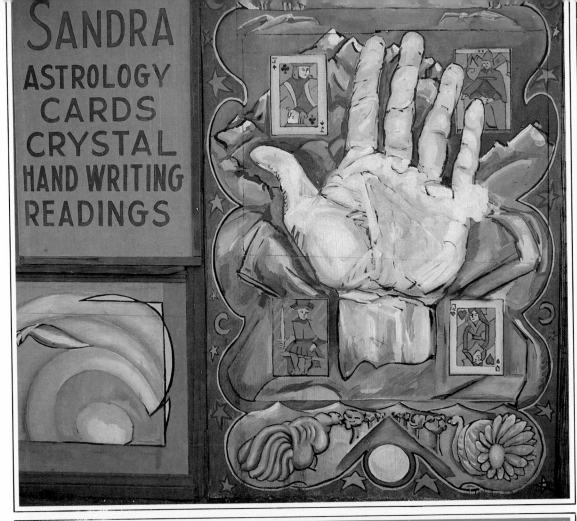

SANDRA
ASTROLOGY
CARDS
CRYSTAL
HAND WRITING
READINGS

Disneyland is Walt Disney's "Magic Kingdom" *these pages.* Built on 150 acres, it is a cornucopia of fantasy and adventure where everyone can live in a child's make-believe world.

Lovely Mission San Carlos Borromeo de Carmelo *bottom left and bottom right.* In Pacific Grove can be seen Green Gables Inn *left. Below and opposite page* above San Simeon on "The Enchanted Hill" stands the domain created by William Randolph Hearst, and here can be seen the Greek Temple imported from Europe, alongside a Romanesque pool.

Soft curves of sand dunes *opposite page* sweep across Death Valley, with the hard ridges of its mountains on the horizon. Also to be found in legendary Death Valley National Monument is Artist's Palette *above* where colors formed by oxidation lie splashed across the hillside.

The labyrinthine landscape of Death Valley displays an astonishing diversity of form and nature. Golden Canyon *above* and the scene from Zabriskie Point *opposite page,* which is an area of lake beds dating back 5 to 10 million years.

Death Valley National Monument, where ragged salt deposits
cover Devils Golf Course *opposite page*. Ubehebe Crater
above is about 500 feet deep and half a mile across.
Ubehebe, formed by a volcanic explosion some 3,000 years
ago, means "big basket" in Shoshone.

Sea, wind and rain have conspired to carve out the raw and rugged coastline at Point Lobos *above* where waves surge over the rocks to explode in foam and form eddying swirls with the sea's endless surge. Gray Whale Cove *opposite page*, north of Montara, with its unspoilt beach.

The coastline of California is at its rugged best along Big Sur, Monterey County. Waves roll against the rocks *top left* as the sun sinks into Pacific seas. In the Pebble Beach area, the famous golf course there provides wonderful sport, especially at the 7th hole *left and above*. *Top* a silver sheen sparkles from the waters at Bixby Creek Bridge.

Opposite page: top right deserted Garra Pata Creek with verdant foliage tumbling down the slope alongside the glistening stream. *Bottom right* Monterey daytime mist hazes the horizon where the colors are blue of sky and deeper blue of sea, giving way to land of undulating green. *Left* the sun sets in flaming gold over Monterey Harbor.

Cabrillo Highway *above* runs along the Californian
coastline south of Carmel, below folded hills dwarfing the
works of man. Along the coast, on Highway 1, is Bixby
Creek Bridge *opposite page* which arcs over in a graceful
span 260 feet above the water.

The Pebble Beach area of the Monterey Peninsula is one of outstanding beauty. Here there are three famous golf courses, each near to ocean and forest: Spyglass Hill, Cypress Point *opposite page* and Pebble Beach *above*, its sixth and seventh holes observed from the air.

Black and heavy storm clouds blot out the sun's rays *above* at Point Sur. The sun bejewels the sea *opposite page* at China Cove, Point Lobos State Reserve. The cove is part of a protected promontory of 1,250 acres and enfolds the only beach safe for swimmers.

On the foreshore of Carmel Beach gnarled cypress trees frame two strollers on the sand. Because of the hazardous surf it is not really a swimming beach, although it is a pleasant place to while away the day, especially early in the morning or late afternoon.

The Lone Cypress *opposite page* stands a solitary sentinel at Sunset Point, Monterey. At Point Lobos *below* a skeletal tree rears upwards from the cliff's edge like a stag's multi-pointed antlers, with the sea beyond churned to froth against sun-dappled rocks.

Big Sur and Monterey Peninsula's coastline is studded by
crags and rocks along the salt sea strand. Mist softens
the outline of these stony masses *above* which have proven
to be the ruin of many a ship on its way towards safe
harbor in Monterey Bay.

After leaving Carmel, Highway 1 curves and dips through
Big Sur country, side-winding over a land offering
timeless, deep-blue visions of the Pacific Ocean below.
At Bixby Creek *these pages* a mighty span of bridge links
the chasm's walls.

Golden Gate Park, San Francisco, is a tribute to William Hall – the first park engineer – and Superintendent John McLaren, who helped to tame 3 miles of shifting sand dunes to create the tranquillity and graceful beauty that is there today. It is an impressive park with many attractions, including the Buddha statue *right* and the Japanese Tea Gardens *below*. *Far right* mighty redwoods, ancient beyond the span of mortal man's years, straddle a footpath in Muir Woods National Monument.

Opposite page: looking south from Mission Dolores Park lies the predominantly Latin area, with Downtown San Francisco dominating the skyline.

In the Mission District, colourful murals *above* brighten many walls and fences. On the streets, flamboyant characters *right and top center* give the area a joyous individuality to everday city life. *Opposite page:* seen from the St Francis Hotel, Union Square is a patch of lushness surrounded by the Downtown towerblocks. Here on sunny lunchtimes, 'brown-baggers' gather from the nearby offices and shops.

Symbol of the city, the Golden Gate Bridge was completed in 1937, reaching across the bay in graceful spans, linking San Francisco with the hills of Marin County to the north. The waters below the bridge sparkle azure in the sunshine and sailing craft can find safe haven in a nearby marina *opposite page*. Others prefer to ride the waves on surf-boards *above* and where the spume rises around the rocky coastline seals *right* find a natural haven.

San Francisco is the only city in the
world with a cable car system in
current operation *left and top*.
Crawling along, the cable cars still
carry up to 25,000 passengers a day in
summer. *Opposite page:* the glorious
Sheraton-Palace Hotel's Garden Court.

The conservatory in Golden Gate Park *above and top* contains within its humid atmosphere a riot of tropical colors among the floral exotica. A remnant of the Victorian era, the building, manufactured in New York, was shipped to the West Coast via the straits of Cape Horn. In the park's Japanese Tea Garden *right* an ornamental pool displays a pavilion's reflection, its intricacy echoed in the nearby bridge.

Bright lights and neon signs pulse out their message of fast-living and eager love into the Broadway night. The fabled Barbary Coast caters to every pleasure-seeker with 'bucks to burn' as the bars, restaurants and clubs, all anxious to lure the tourist towards them, proclaim the delights that await inside.

The city of San Francisco is surrounded by water on three sides. Hence there is a great amount of focus on the sea for work and sport. Fisherman's Wharf *left, top left and opposite page* is where many of the local fishermen land their catch and the area has produced some very fine seafood restaurants as a result of the fresh sea-haul. *Above* Coit Tower, its shape designed to resemble a firehose nozzle, stands high on Telegraph Hill looking down from its lofty position to the wharf below.

This page: brightly painted weatherboarded houses give the older section of this city unique character. Each salient feature has been underscored by the use of contrasting color. However, many fine structures similar to these are falling slowly into disrepair and will eventually be destroyed.
Opposite page: in one of San Francisco's early residential areas a motley collection of houses lies checkered over the hilly landscape.

Overleaf: left the shimmering of the sea contrasts strongly with the fall of the black-shrouded night sky as power, sail and free-flying gull race homewards to the land's embrace. *Right* morning mist floats the city above a grey sea, the sweep of the suspension bridge cutting across the clouds.

Dusk descends and the daytime workers in San Fransico's
Downtown region bustle homewards by tram, car and train.
Above and opposite page, left Powell Street undulates upwards
to the historic heights of Nob Hill. *Opposite page, right*
the sun has bleached out all color to black and white.

The University of Berkeley *right* is almost a self-contained town and the oldest campus in California. Stanford University was founded in 1883 by railroad baron Leland Stanford. It is graced by red-tiled roofs *below*, perfect rounds of Romanesque-style arches *bottom left and bottom right* and the most exquisite stained glass *opposite page*.

Chinatown sprawls over 24 blocks of San Francisco and contains the largest Chinese community outside of Asia. Drawn here originally in gold rush days, this ethnic group originally remained close-knit against exploitation and persecution and today their language, religion and customs still endure.

Grant Avenue *opposite page* is a very busy, but narrow thoroughfare bisecting Chinatown from north to south. The colors and odors permeate the senses with a feel of the Orient as one strolls along the sidewalk in this vibrant area.

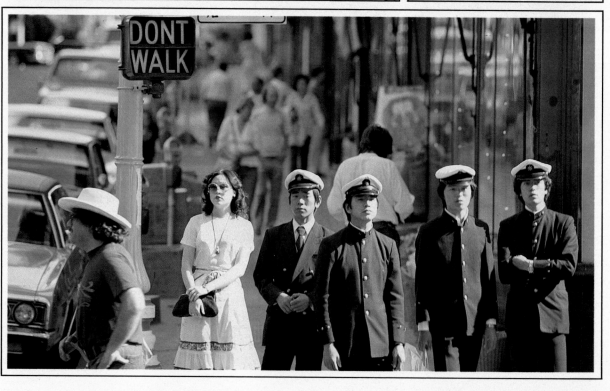

Claiming to be the most crooked street in the world, Lombard Street *this page* changes direction ten times as it snakes past well-tended gardens on Russian Hill, between Hyde and Leavenworth. *Opposite page:* Coit Tower and the Transamerica Building stand on the skyline looking down on Fisherman's Wharf where boats ride at their moorings.

On any day of the year boats, ships and yachts criss-cross this natural harbor, safe haven against the tumult of the ocean's might. A container ship *opposite page* dwarfs a sailing craft off its starboard bow.

A graceful, old building *far left* stands in the shadows of the taller structures of a newer age. Weatherboarded houses *left* line a deserted backstreet. *Below and bottom center* holding on tight as the cable car rides along the streets. Fort Point *bottom left,* officially known as Fort William Scott, was built in 1861 under the southern arch of the Golden Gate Bridge as part of a chain of similar forts built in the 1800s to guard the seacoast of the United States. However, its 127 cannons have never been fired in anger. During World Wars I and II, German prisoners were housed there, but today one can wander freely through this monolith.

Opposite page: these lovely old houses have retained their unique architectural charms even though many years have gone past since they were first designed.

A cobweb of latticework against the pastel evening sky, the steel cables, girders and massive pillars of the Golden Gate Bridge trace their way across the sweep of the bay. A burning ball of flame *bottom* stains the scene a reddish hue with a gilded path over the waters. A lone yacht *opposite page* sails homewards over a sea of shimmering silver, the silhouetted and rocky headland safely passed by to port.

Frozen moments in time: a jogger *left* is caught
by the camera's eye in mid-stride on the brow of
the hill; justice being dispensed *above* and
boarding the cable car *top*. *Opposite page:* time
is stretched as a long exposure records the
signature of red tail-lights.

A cable car is turned manually *left* at the foot of Powell Street, prior to its next ascent towards Nob Hill. The spire of the Transamerica Building *below* seems symbolic of the high-towered Downtown area, seen *opposite page* in a hue of pale green from a myriad office lights.
Overleaf: left the flat-topped roofs of these older buildings form a strong contrast to the perpendicular walls of the skyscrapers; above the friendly glow of their living rooms the luminous, pyramidal spike of the Transamerica Building sears the Californian sky. *Right* twilight and city-lights have incarnadined the San Francisco vista as cars scurry homewards across the Golden Gate Bridge.

Succulent and tempting, these displays of fish and roasted duck hang in the shop windows of Chinatown. The evening will bring many people here to sample the delights of tasty Chinese cuisine in restaurants set amid the atmospheric streets.

The San Francisco-Oakland Bay Bridge was completed in the 1930s, effectively ending the bay's ferry boat era, although some people still prefer the boat trip to the drive across the bridge in rush-hour traffic. The suspension and cantilever section are both double-decked to allow for a constant stream of traffic.

The Napa Valley *above* is in the very heart of Californian wine country. Come September and golden October these vineyards will be ripe for harvesting. In the High Sierras *opposite page* a cowboy and his horse pick their way round gilded trees and a lapis lazuli lake.

This page: the Napa Valley, just north of San Francisco, produces fine grapes *above* and is synonymous with 'The Wine Country'. The huge casks *below* are in the winery of the Christian Brothers. Traditional architectural style of the region *left* set among magnificent surroundings.

Opposite page: the buildings of Bodie are now part of a State Historic Park. Once it was a booming gold mining town with a far-flung notoriety. When at its peak, this 'den of iniquity' supported 65 saloons and there was also an average of one murder a day.

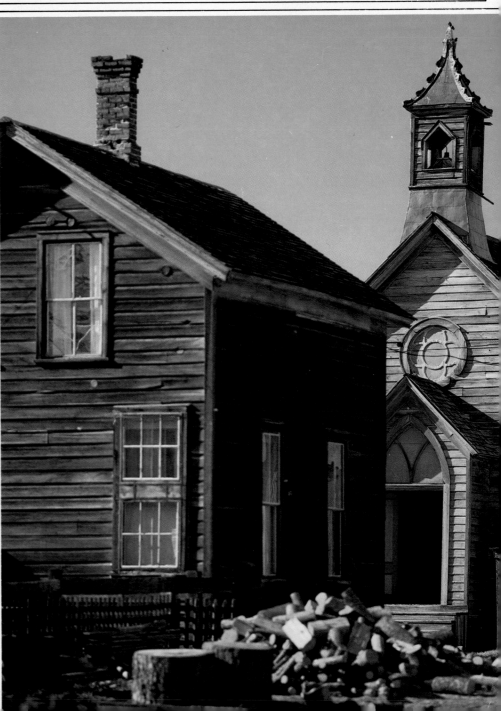

Kings Canyon *above* in all its massive grandeur. At the
end of Yosemite Valley cascades Bridalveil Falls *opposite
page*. It impresses not through size or power but by sheer
spectacular beauty, set as it is among graceful domes and
granite cliffs.

Tenaya Canyon *opposite page* still bears the scars of
Nature's glacial might which aeons ago split the rocks and
scoured the gorge as if with a pumice stone. The still
and quiet Mirror Lake *above* echoes the squat bulk of Mount
Watkins.

Upper Yosemite Valley *above* seen from Glacier Point.
Opposite page: in Yosemite National Park can also be seen
the waterfalls called Nevada and Vernal. They are the
upper and lower falls in the photograph respectively,
appearing diminutive within this panoramic splendor.

Described by naturalist John Muir as a "Range of Light",
the Sierra Nevada *these pages* is the largest single chain
of mountains in the country. An electric blue stream of
melt water *above* plunges irresistibly downwards. *Right* a
cerulean lake ringed by remnants of winter's icey grip.

Hat Creek *above* rushes between verdant banks through
Lassen Volcanic National Park. An uprooted tree in mid-
stream is etched by the constant flow of the water in
flood. Isolated trees do find a foothold, however, in the
lava beds *opposite page* known as the 'Painted Dunes'.

Volcanic Lassen Peak *above* looks down upon ice-blotched
Lake Helen. Bumpass Hell *opposite page* in Lassen Volcanic
National Park still displays the action of geological
forces as sulphur pools, boiling mud pots and clouds of
steam vent from the volatile earth.

Emerald Bay *opposite page* lies near the south end of Lake
Tahoe, the "Jewel of the Sierra" which is 22 miles long by
8 to 12 miles wide, offering space and sport for all. A
pool of bubbling mud *above* in Lassen Volcanic National
Park's Bumpass Hell.

It is not only the giant sequoias that should be seen in
Sequoia National Park. Monarch Lakes, Rainbow Mountain
and Mineral Peak *above. Opposite page:* the lonely
magnificence of Columbine Lake and Lost Canyon. *Overleaf:*
Lombard Street, San Francisco, at night.